SELL YOUR BOOK on **Amazon**

SECOND EDITION

Top-Secret Tips **Guaranteed** to
Increase Sales for Print-on-Demand
and Self-Publishing Writers

SECOND EDITION

BRENT SAMPSON

Foreword by Dan Poynter

Outskirts Press, Inc.
Denver, Colorado

Sell Your Book on Amazon
Top-Secret Tips Guaranteed to Increase Sales for Print-On-Demand and Self-Publishing Writers
SECOND EDITION
All Rights Reserved
Copyright © 2007, 2010 Outskirts Press, Inc.

Outskirts Press
http://www.outskirtspress.com

ISBN-10: 1-4327-0196-7
ISBN-13: 978-1-4327-0196-3

Library of Congress Control Number: 2006940383

Outskirts Press and the "OP" logo are trademarks belonging to
Outskirts Press, Inc.

Printed in the United States of America

CONTENTS

Bookstores are a lousy place to sell books.

- Dan Poynter

FOREWORD

BY DAN POYNTER

Amazon is changing the book industry. What used to be possible for only a statistical few is now available for everybody. If you have a book, Amazon makes it possible to reach a worldwide audience almost effortlessly.

Of course, reaching that worldwide audience and selling to them is where "effortlessly" just doesn't cut it anymore. In spite of your having immediate access to one of the largest audiences of motivated buyers, selling a book successfully on Amazon requires work. But it is work almost anyone can do and excel at if the proper techniques are employed.

> If you have a book, Amazon makes it possible to reach a worldwide audience almost effortlessly.

Unlike speaking or making public appearances on television or at bookstores, selling on Amazon does not require you to be an extrovert, not even occasionally. You do not have to be a beautiful presenter, or even presentably beautiful. You can sell your book in your sweat suit just as successfully as in your three-piece suit.

I travel around the world as a speaker. I sell thousands of books in BOR "back of the room sales" and I love what I do. Amazon sales are a nice complement but do not represent my primary income. Public speaking still plays the largest role in my success. To breathe motivation into an author on the cusp of publication breathes life into me. My purpose in speaking is to impart knowledge.

But public speaking is not for everyone. Introverts rejoice! Amazon.com represents a worldwide platform from which you can shout to the world (in your underwear if you wish), "I am a published author! Buy my book with a click of a button!"

Whether or not anyone hears you depends upon your familiarity with the techniques described in this book. Now you can benefit from publishing executive Brent Sampson's firsthand experience with many authors' successes and failures. As the presi-

Amazon.com represents a worldwide platform from which you can shout to the world, "I am a published author! Buy my book!"

dent of Outskirts Press, he witnesses authors earning between zero and tens of thousands of dollars a month in royalties. In almost all cases, the difference between those two extremes is Amazon.

I first met Brent Sampson via email when he requested a cover blurb for his book *Publishing Gems*. We later met physically when I was in Denver speaking to the Colorado Independent Publishers Association. He handed me a copy of *Publishing Gems* with my quotation on it. The fact that the majority of communication in our initial exchange occurred virtually serves as a testament to the power of the Internet.

It is no longer uncommon for entire books to be collaborated on, published, distributed, and sold without one single face-to-face meeting! In fact, it is more common than not. Of the approximately 200,000 books published each year in America, the majority of them are published via email, phone, and the Internet.

Say good-bye to rush-hour commutes to your publisher and last-minute press checks at two in the morning. Now your time can be better spent writing your next book and promoting your current one. The Internet is revolutionizing publishing. Leading the charge is Amazon, which serves as

> In almost all cases, the difference between $0 per month and $10,000 per month in royalties is Amazon.

a publicist, marketing firm, distributor, and retailer all in one. You can reap the benefits of this book-selling dynamo without ever leaving your house—and can save a pretty penny in the process.

Yes, time is money, and to truly benefit from these pages, you need to invest quite a bit of time. And yes, money is money; some tactics in this book have a price tag. But sum up the cost of hiring a publicist or marketing firm, and you will realize the savings offered between the covers of this book cannot be measured.

There may be terms in this book that are foreign to you—"wiki," "plog," and "tag," for example. In fact, these terms are so new that their very definitions are in a state of flux. Such is the dynamic nature of the Internet. This fluidity represents a particular challenge when trying to describe the step-by-step tactics involved in promoting a book online.

It's not unlike taking a photograph of a locomotive with a telephoto lens. It may be a little blurry, but reach through the surface material and dig to the basic marketing concepts found within. You will be rewarded: impressions, conversions, and ROI (return on investment). These concepts are marketing mainstays, even if they are the last

> Terms like "wiki," "plog," and "tag" are so new that their very definitions are in a state of flux.

millennium's "wiki," "plog," and "tag" idioms. Remembering what book publishing was like in the 20th century is for historians. Acting upon what publishing is like today, right now, is for writers.

Which are you?

Dan Poynter
The Self-Publishing Manual
Santa Barbara, Calif.

A brand for a company is like a reputation for a person. You earn reputation by trying to do hard things well.

- *Jeff Bezos*

INTRODUCTION
AMAZON: A BRIEF HISTORY

Amazon was founded by Jeff Bezos and opened for business on the World Wide Web in July of 1995. From the beginning, Bezos's vision was to create the most customer-centric company in the world.

What does *customer-centric* mean?

- Figure out what your customers want and deliver it.
- Use technical innovation to find out what customers do not even know they want, and deliver that, too.
- Personalize each online shopping experience for each and every individual customer.

While Amazon performs all three of these tasks remarkably well, it is the second and third bullet points that offer the greatest opportunity to the online book marketer.

Goal #2 introduces new products to pre-qualified shoppers; goal #3 creates a personal shopping experience based upon previous habits. These two components work synergistically to create an amazing online marketing opportunity.

TACTIC RANKING SYSTEM

Sell Your Book on Amazon shows you how to leverage Amazon's company goals to your own advantage. Ultimately, marketing advice is only as valuable as the profit it generates.

Profitability is more than just the accumulation of dollars and cents. It is the comparison between your investment and your return on that investment.

Every tactic in this book requires only an investment of time. The return on investment (ROI) that you earn by following these tactics is an analysis only you can make.

To assist in that analysis I have concocted the following ranking system:

Tactics with five stars are highly recommend-   ★★★★★
ed. If the steps are followed as prescribed,
you are likely to receive the greatest amount
of exposure for your book in relation to the
investment made.

Tactics with four stars are recommended but   ★★★★
they may require a larger investment and the
payoff may either be smaller or slower.

The investment of time and/or money for three-   ★★★
star tactics is so great that even the return may
pale in comparison, depending upon your profit
margin.

The tactics in this book are designed to help   ★★
you, so you may only see two stars to point
out pursuits you should consider very carefully.

One-star tactics should be avoided, unless   ★
unusual circumstances apply.

Keep in mind that these marketing rankings are generalizations. Every book is different. What may be a one-star tactic for some
may very well be a five-star tactic for others.

Problems cannot be solved
at the same level of awareness
that created them.

- *Albert Einstein*

CHAPTER 1

GET LISTED

Before you can sell your book on Amazon, your book must be listed on Amazon. There is an easy way to accomplish this and there is a hard way. Let us examine the advantages and disadvantages of both.

THE HARD WAY

The hard way involves Amazon's Advantage program. While even the hard method is relatively straightforward, it is not as simple as the easy method that will be covered later.

An ISBN is the unique identifying number for your book. Like Social Security numbers or snowflakes, no two ISBNs are alike.

In order to be eligible for Amazon Advantage, you must acquire an ISBN (International Standard Book Number) for your book. ISBNs are like Social Security numbers or snowflakes—no two are alike. Basically, the ISBN is your book's Social Security number. It is the unique identifying number for your book. Amazon needs the ISBN for inventory and accounting purposes. Since different books can share a title but not an ISBN, ISBNs are used throughout the publishing industry for unique book identification.

If you are an independently self-published author, you may or may not already have an ISBN for your book. If you don't, you will need to get one. Typically, if you published through a traditional publisher or a print-on-demand publisher, you received an ISBN with your publication.

If you do not have an ISBN, you can get one from the U.S. ISBN Agency, Bowker, for $125. Their website for purchasing unique ISBNs is **www.myidentifiers.com.** Purchasing your own ISBN from the ISBN Agency recognizes you as the publisher of record.

Once you have an ISBN, you will also need a bar code. The bar code is the scannable graphic on the back of most book covers. Like the ISBN, the bar code is used for inventory management. Computers use the bar code to scan books quickly in order to determine inventory levels and sales numbers.

The ISBN Agency will sell you a bar code for each ISBN that you acquire for a slightly higher fee. Or you can find third-party service providers who create bar codes by request. You provide the ISBN and retail price, and in return, you receive a bar code, usually in the form of a high-resolution graphic such as a TIFF or JPEG file.

Fig. 1 - www.amazon.com/advantage

Once you have copies of your book with an ISBN and bar code, visit **www.amazon.com/advantage** to apply for the Amazon Advantage program. Review their contractual terms carefully. Basically, you accept that their annual fee ($29.95 at the time of this writing) is nonrefundable and their commission is 55% of your retail price.

Once you are accepted into the Amazon Advantage program, have paid their fees, and have accepted their 55% margin requirement, your book has the opportunity to be listed like any traditionally published or on-demand published book, with its own Amazon listing. I will refer to a book's listing on Amazon as the Book Detail Page.

I say it has the *opportunity* to be listed like traditional or on-demand titles because completing your listing through Amazon Advantage requires further work on your end. Simply listing your book for sale is different from having an optimal Book Detail Page. Suffice it to say that just being a part of the Amazon Advantage program does not necessarily mean you have all of those things taken care of for you. You still need to upload your cover image and book description, set your subject categories (BISAC codes), and complete all the elements of your Book Detail Page.

Chapter Three thoroughly discusses the Book Detail Page and covers all the steps that should be followed to make your listing on Amazon as effective as possible.

Chapter Three thoroughly discusses the Book Detail Page and covers all the steps that should be followed to make your listing on Amazon as effective as possible in selling your book.

Your next step is mailing copies of your book to Amazon at your cost. Amazon notifies you via email whenever you need to send more books. You might mail one or two books to begin with. In a couple of months or a couple of weeks, depending upon the demand for your book, they will contact you and request more. The quantity depends upon the demand for your book. Amazon strives to keep between two and three weeks of inventory in its warehouse at any given time. The quantity of orders you receive reflects your sales trend.

You may find yourself sending two or three copies to Amazon at a time, or you may find yourself sending a case of books. It depends upon your marketing initiatives and how popular your book is. You always pay for shipping and you cannot control the number of copies Amazon orders at a time.

Consider your long-term profitability with the Amazon Advantage program carefully. If your book has a suggested retail price of $10.00, Amazon makes $5.50 for every sale; you make $4.50. Since you are also responsi-

> Amazon strives to keep between two and three weeks of inventory in its warehouse at any given time. The quantity of orders you receive reflects your sales trend.

ble for shipping books to Amazon and printing those books in the first place, you must
account for the shipping and production
costs when determining your profitability.

To be truly accurate, you must account for
the cost of shipping your books twice: once
from the printer to your storage facility—
usually your garage—and then again to Amazon. Plus, you need to consider the number of
hours spent packing up copies of your book
and mailing them to Amazon in response to
orders. That $4.50 gross may become $1.00
net once all associated costs are considered.
You will find further discussion about pricing
in the last chapter of this book.

★★★★★   ## THE EASY WAY

The easy method involves publishing
through a company rather than independently publishing it yourself. There are a number
of ways to accomplish this.

You can submit your book to a traditional publisher such as Random House.
The publisher may take three to six months
to consider your proposal and another one
or two years to publish your book if they
accept it. The good news is, once they accept your book, they will take care of all

the Amazon steps for you. Of course, marketing is an exercise *all* successful authors partake in; you still want to read the rest of this book.

Traditional publishers accept a very low percentage of books. More often than not, their marketing department makes the final decision. Basically, if a traditional publisher accepts your book, it means they think it is marketable. Well, in that case, you might as well publish it yourself and keep more of the money, right?

That's where POD (print-on-demand) publishing comes in. This is the easiest way to get your book listed on Amazon. By printing or publishing your book through a company with a direct EDI link to Amazon, such as any number of POD author services and book publishing providers, your book will typically meet all the requirements set forth by the Amazon Advantage program. The on-demand printer or publisher can usually take care of the remaining details of getting your book listed on Amazon for you, provided they use EDI (electronic data interchange) distribution methods. We will cover EDI in greater detail later.

Before choosing an on-demand printer or publisher, do your homework. Not all companies are the same and they each offer dif-

> If a traditional publisher accepts your book, it means they think it is marketable. You might as well market it yourself and keep more of the money.

ferent advantages. You want to find a company that distributes through both Ingram and Baker & Taylor, one that lets you keep all the rights to your book, and one that offers a non-exclusive contract.

For independently published authors who have chosen not to pursue the traditional route or the convenience of print-on-demand, the Amazon Advantage program and its 55% margin may seem like the only recourse. Fortunately, there is another option for self-published authors sitting on a pile of printed books. A growing number of authors are publishing an "on-demand edition" of their book to take advantage of the convenience and services afforded by POD and EDI.

In this case, you still have an offset print run that you sell the same way as always—through direct sales, niche markets, and non-exclusive distributors or regional wholesalers.

Simultaneously, you can publish an on-demand edition that distributes through Ingram's EDI feed. Your book is then listed online with Amazon and Barnes & Noble through their EDI distribution partnerships. Online sales of your book are received, printed, and fulfilled independently of your involvement and inventory. The listings do not stop with Amazon and Barnes & Noble.

Online sales of your book are received, printed, and fulfilled independently of your involvement and inventory.

Any online retailer with a direct EDI feed to Ingram is usually included in the network. This typically includes Borders.com, Powells.com, the website for Books-A-Million, etc. In fact, it is not uncommon for authors using an on-demand publisher or printer to suddenly find their books for sale on sites like eBay, much to their delight!

To successfully publish an on-demand edition simultaneously with an offset version, be sure that you choose a company that lets you use your own ISBN and imprint name if you so choose. Very few offer this level of flexibility, so that will help narrow down your choices.

Some print-on-demand printers and publishers even offer the flexibility to secure Amazon listings for considerably less than 55% discounts, which means more money in your pocket! In many cases, this increased profit margin compensates for the higher per-unit costs typically associated with print-on-demand publishing. Chapter Seven discusses *short discounting* your way to higher profits.

The successful warrior is the
average man with laser-like focus.

- Bruce Lee

CHAPTER 2

AUTHOR CENTRAL & AMAZON PROFILES

Once your book is listed on Amazon for sale, your next step involves the creation of an Author Central (previously AuthorConnect) account and completing your Author Profile Page.

Author Central was still in beta as I was writing this, so it may have changed a little bit since this edition was published.

AUTHOR CENTRAL   ★★★★★

Your Author Central account is a supplement to your regular Amazon account that you use to purchase products. If you do not have an Amazon account yet, what are you waiting for? You must have an Amazon account to promote your book successfully on Amazon, and it needs to be a verified, valid account. That means, as far as Amazon is concerned, you need to buy something from them using an approved credit or debit card.

You also need to create an Author Central account. Do that here: **www.amazon. com/authors**.

Once you are signed in to your Author Central account, you can modify your bibliography from the "Books" tab, upload a photo and biography from the "Profile" tab, compose a blog from the "Blog" tab, upload a video from the "Video" tab, and add a calendar of events from the "Events" tab.

Previous to the creation of Author Central, which is new to Amazon as of 2009, the information detailed under the "Books," "Profile," and "Blog" tabs were maintained under the Amazon Profile section.

Now there are two profiles you need to maintain: the one in Author Central, and the one in Amazon. The first controls your Author Page, and the second controls your "platform" on Amazon.

Both are important to keep professional and up-to-date, although the latter has more direct relevancy to the topics (and benefits) discussed in this book, so that's where we will concentrate our focus.

AMAZON PROFILE

Updating your Amazon Profile is different from updating your Author Central account. To access your Amazon Profile, sign in to your normal Amazon account and then access your Amazon Profile Page. Amazon does not make it easy to find. The quickest way is to click on the "recommendations" link at the very top of the page where Amazon greets you by name. Your recommendations page is updated dynamically based upon your recent purchases and activity. You will see a series of sub-tabs under the search bar. The third button from the right says, **Your Profile.** Click it to review and modify your Author Profile Page.

Like all things on Amazon, there is an easy way and a hard way. The method described above is the hard way. The easy way is to access your Amazon Profile Page directly at **www.amazon.com/gp/pdp.** If you have your cookies activated, it will take you straight to your profile.

The difficulty in discussing the Amazon Profile Page (or just about any page, for that matter) is due to Amazon's dynamic nature. Every user sees something slightly different. That fact contributes to Amazon's appeal, but also makes it difficult to summarize in published text. Bear in mind that what I describe is based upon my own user experience and will relate to your experience only in a general sense.

Fig. 2 - www.amazon.com/gp/pdp

For example, your own Amazon Profile Page will be different from this screenshot because yours will depend upon the information you have provided to Amazon. Recognize the generalities in this book and then apply specifics as necessary.

AUTHOR PHOTO & CAPTION

My personal profile page greets me with the words: "Brent Sampson's Profile, OutskirtsPress.com CEO." There is a picture of me along the left-hand side, and underneath the picture, it says, "Brent Sampson, President/CEO of Outskirts Press, Inc. at www.OutskirtsPress.com."

If your Amazon Profile does not display your photograph, you should upload one. If you had a professional picture taken for the back of your book, you probably received the appropriate permissions to include it elsewhere, including on Amazon.

On the other hand, if the photograph on your book cover was taken by a family member in your backyard, you may want to forego it altogether. Or better yet, have a professional photograph taken. A professional photograph is always preferable. If your Amazon image matches the photograph on the back of your book(s), you are taking the first step toward branding yourself. An author's brand is very important for success. Often, nonfiction writers brand their subject matter (*South Beach Diet*), while fiction authors most commonly brand their names (Stephen King).

Every time somebody sees you in association with your book, they should see the same image. As anybody who works on Madison Avenue will tell you, repetition is key.

To modify your profile, you must first click the **Edit Profile** button. Then, to add or edit your photograph, click on the link under the photo that says **Change photo & Caption**. Amazon provides the opportunity to browse the contents of your hard drive for a photograph you want to use. Below the **Browse** button is another input field for supplying the caption to your photograph.

The caption represents a great opportunity for promotion. In most cases, you will want to mention the title of your book. But you can market anything, even a company name or website. Make sure to mention something that benefits you or your book, since many of the tactics in this book are designed to drive potential customers to your Amazon Profile Page for more information. The photograph you use and the caption

The caption represents a great opportunity for promotion. Make sure to mention something that benefits you or your book, since potential customers will visit your Author Profile Page often.

underneath it should instill confidence and motivate purchases of your product.

Amazon.com allows domain names and company names in certain areas and not in others. You should take advantage of the places where Amazon does allow domain names, but only if you have a domain name to promote. If you have a product that you sell from your website, then you might want to use Amazon to get people to look at your website.

If you sell only books from your website, and if your profits are equal to or less than what you make from Amazon (remember to keep in mind the time spent fulfilling those orders personally), then there is little point in directing people away from Amazon just to buy your book elsewhere. Your caption should mention the one thing you want people to know about you. Most of the time, that "one thing" is the title of your book.

Since the caption for my photograph includes a domain name instead of a book title, let me make a general comment before we proceed with the next section. Using your Amazon caption to promote your website is valuable only if your website contributes to your bottom line. After all, if you are reading *Sell Your Book on Amazon* and following its advice, you probably plan on selling your book

> Your caption should mention the one thing you want people to know about you. Most of the time, that "one thing" is the title of your book.

on Amazon. To that end, your best use of the caption space most likely includes the title of your book. It can even duplicate your Amazon signature, which you provide in the "About Me" section, below.

★★★★★   **ABOUT ME**

Below your photograph is the "About Me" section. Here is where you see and edit all your personal details. Do not forget that other people who visit your Author Profile Page will see some of this information, too. The point is to make your biography contribute to your overall sales goals.

The first piece of information is your name. This should consistently be the same name under which you write all your books.

The second piece of information is your "Personal Headline." Amazon calls it the "Signature," but since that name is easily confused with the signature you use in your reviews, for example, I will be referring to this component of your profile as the Personal Headline throughout this book. Your Personal Headline on Amazon is a way to brand yourself with a succinct and notable catchphrase or *hook*. It needs to "accomplish something" in a finite amount of space.

In my case, my Personal Headline says, "President/CEO of OutskirtsPress.com" at the time of this writing, although it has changed words and length numerous times. At all times, however, it establishes who I am in a professional sense while building credibility. It always refers to either our publishing company, our website domain, or my publications. As with the photo caption, you always want your Personal Headline to mention something compelling, so that when people see it on Amazon, they are motivated to click on it to visit your Amazon Profile Page. That is where you get to mention more about yourself and your books. Often, the photo caption and Personal Headline may match.

It is equally important for your Personal Headline to establish your expertise in your category. If you have written a cookbook, your Headline should indicate that you wrote a book because you have the credentials to do so. People buy nonfiction books from experts. Since most of my books are about writing, publishing, and marketing books, my stature as the president/CEO of a publishing company fortifies that expert status.

Amazon includes your Headline with much of your online activity, so it is important to come up with a great Personal Headline. Every

Every review you write, wiki you create, and product you tag includes your Headline. Your Headline will be everywhere on Amazon. It represents you.

review you write, wiki you create, and product you tag includes your Headline, which links to your Profile. In other words, your Personal Headline will be *everywhere* on Amazon and it represents you. That is a good thing, especially if the Headline mentions something of value (such as your book title).

The third piece of information in the "About Me" section is your location, which is self-explanatory.

The fourth piece of information is your reviewer rank. The more book reviews you write, the higher your rank and the lower your number. If you write enough reviews, Amazon identifies you as a Top 1000 Reviewer, Top 500 Reviewer, Top 50 Reviewer, Top 10 Reviewer, or #1 Reviewer. Yes, you should strive to reach this status.

Below your reviewer rank is a link to the number of reviews you have written. Clicking that link takes you to all your reviews. Simply put, you want to write as many reviews as possible, concentrating on books that are similar to, or in direct competition with, yours.

Do not universally criticize these books. Instead, give them accurate reviews in a positive manner. There is very little benefit to giving a book a poor review, since the whole point in writing the review is getting people

> The more book reviews you write, the higher your reviewer rank and the lower your number. If you write enough reviews, Amazon identifies you as a ranked reviewer.

to click on your Personal Headline. The better the reviews, the more people will see
your Headline and, therefore, click on it. You
want these books to sell. Your review should
be applicable and contribute to the overall
content of that book's Detail Page. Remember, these are not anonymous reviews. Your
Headline is going to accompany your review
and you want people to react positively to
your opinion. I will cover reviews in more
depth later on in this chapter and in Chapter
Three.

> Write as many reviews as possible, concentrating on books that are similar to yours.

The fifth piece of information in the
"About Me" section covers your Listmania
Lists. It displays the number of times your
lists have been seen, how many lists you
have created, and how helpful your lists are
to other people. You want all these numbers
to be high, particularly the number of times
your lists have been viewed.

Of course, the more lists you have, the
more people are likely to see them. Creating Listmania Lists is very important to your
overall Amazon tactics. Therefore, I discuss
Listmania in greater detail in Chapter Four.

The sixth piece of information in the
"About Me" section covers your Amazon
Guides or, more accurately (albeit awk-
wardly), your "So You'd Like To...Guides."
As with Listmania, your Amazon Profile dis-

plays the number of times your guides have been viewed, how many guides you have written, and how helpful your guides are to others. Amazon Guides present a valuable marketing opportunity in their own right, so I discuss them in greater detail in Chapter Five.

The seventh, eighth, and ninth pieces of information concern your customer images, email address, and website address—all relatively self-explanatory.

Your biography comes next. You may edit it along with all your personal details by clicking the **Edit** link directly below the words "About Me" at the top of the section.

Consider your biography very carefully before composing it. The biography must accomplish a number of things while still fitting completely within the finite amount of space reserved for it on your Amazon Profile Page. After you write a biography, you may notice Amazon truncate it with the linked word **More** due to lack of space. That tells you the biography is too long and needs to be shortened. People are creatures of habit. They will take the path of least resistance. Why require them to click on a **More** link to see your entire biography when you can make your biography exactly the right length with a little bit of effort?

> Your Amazon biography must accomplish a number of things while still fitting completely within the finite amount of space reserved for it.

Your biography must establish your expertise in your field. It needs to demonstrate that you know how to write competently, without grammatical or spelling errors. If your credentials are important (which they are for every nonfiction book), your biography should include them.

> Your biography must establish your expertise and demonstrate that you can write competently, without grammatical or spelling errors.

Your biography should also mention the title of your book, your company, or your website (or perhaps all three). As you publish more books, your biography should change. Adding or changing your biography indicates that you are growing as a professional.

In fact, it's a good idea to change your Personal Headline from time to time, too. Changes to your Headline and biography maintain your exposure but prevent viewers from becoming complacent when seeing your name.

YOUR LATEST ACTIVITY   ★★★

Under "Contributions," you see the reviews you have written; and under "Interesting People & Friends," you see the network connections you have made. Above "Contributions" you see your "Latest Activity"—that is, if you have done anything on Amazon recently.

In short, Amazon remembers everything you do—everything you buy, everything you look at, every review you write, and every person you make contact with. The purpose, then, is to make sure your activity on Amazon builds upon itself in a productive manner to increase your exposure and further the sales of your book. For example, it is not important who appears on your "Interesting People & Friends" page, but it is important on whose pages you appear!

Let's say you have written a cookbook. Then a chef buys a cookbook on Amazon or writes a review about a cookbook. Perhaps that chef also looks at the author's profile of the cookbook he just purchased. Does he see you listed among that author's "Interesting People & Friends?" If so, perhaps the chef looks at your profile and decides to buy your book, too.

If not, at least know that Amazon will remember his interest in cookbooks based upon his previous cookbook purchase. Therefore, Amazon assumes he might be interested in learning about other cookbooks. Based upon the activity surrounding your cookbook (its ranking, number of reviews, number of comments in your blog, and yes, your networked friendship with that other cookbook author), Amazon may choose to recommend your cookbook to the chef by displaying information about your book on whatever page the chef is viewing. Amazon may even send a recommendation to the chef via email.

This is not random. There is a very distinct algorithm that Amazon uses to put product information in front of its users. All of a sudden, the chef learns about your book based upon a previous purchase he made or activity he completed. When he buys your book, Amazon fulfills its potential, selling a copy of your book to a perfect stranger. You have done nothing more than follow the tactics outlined in this book. Now, multiply that chef by one hundred more.

Yes, it takes effort—but when you have as many people shopping as Amazon has, it is an effort that can pay off.

REVIEWS   ★★★★★

The section above "Interesting People & Friends" displays the reviews you have written, which is directly related to your reviewer ranking. The more reviews you write, the higher your Amazon reviewer ranking climbs.

Writing reviews is time-consuming, but it is time well spent if you do it right. Find time to write as many reviews as you can and post them all on Amazon. Write a review for every book you have read and make time to read more books. The old adage says, "A writer writes!" That's true, but you know what is also true? "A writer reads!"

What is the point of writing reviews? Remember that Amazon attaches your Personal Headline to each review and automatically links it to your Amazon Profile Page, which, in turn, contains promotional elements designed to sell *your* book.

An insightful review is your opportunity to demonstrate to potential customers that you can write professionally and communicate clearly. After all, those are traits readers seek in an author. If customers of similar titles value your review and are interested in the title of your book (conveniently contained in your Personal Headline), they may conduct a search for it on Amazon.

More important than writing reviews for every book you can think of is writing a review for every book within your direct category. Books that share your subject matter also share your potential audience of readers. Similar books and their authors fall within your "competitive network."

A review is your opportunity to demonstrate to potential customers that you can write professionally and clearly.

People interested in your book may stumble upon a competitive book first. Perhaps they have heard of the competitive author, whereas they have not heard of you. That's okay; use this to your advantage. When these shoppers browse the reviews of competitive books they will read your review and see your Headline. They may visit your Amazon Profile, your Author Central Page, and your Book Detail Page, too.

Reviews should not be used as blatant promotional platforms. Each review is subject to removal if enough people indicate that it is abusive. Instead, let your Headline and review speak for themselves, and use the two paragraphs (at least) within the body of your review to demonstrate your proficiency with the English language as you remark intelligently on the book at hand.

The magic number here is one hundred. Plan on writing one hundred reviews within your category to witness some noticeable results. Once you have written one hundred reviews, aim for two hundred, and then five hundred, and then one thousand. Once you are ranked as a Top 1000 reviewer, aim for the next level. Ranked reviewers receive an incredible amount of exposure, particularly reviewers in the Top 50 category, who are pseudo-celebrities in their own right.

> Write a review for every book within your direct category. Books that share your subject matter share your audience of readers.

Have you ever seen a Spotlight Review on Amazon? These are reviews that others have indicated were helpful. Since Spotlight Reviews appear above the normal review section, they are subject to less competition and receive more exposure. So your goal should be to write a lot of *helpful* reviews for a lot of books in your competitive network. A *lot* of helpful votes for a review is what catapults it to the "Spotlight Review" section.

★★★★★   LISTMANIA & AMAZON GUIDES

Listmania and So You'd Like To...Guides receive their own chapters, so I will not cover them in great detail here. Remember these sections of your Amazon Profile Page, however, as they play an important role in the creation and management of your lists and guides when you begin that portion of your book promotion efforts.

If you do not see mention of Listmania Lists or Amazon Guides on your Amazon Profile Page, it means you have not yet created any. We'll discuss how to create them in the following chapters.

I discuss Listmania Lists thoroughly in Chapter Four and Amazon Guides thoroughly in Chapter Five.

INTERESTING PEOPLE & FRIENDS

Amazon is nothing if not duplicative. It recognizes trends in society and adjusts its offerings accordingly. "Interesting People & Friends" takes a page from MySpace, the website that popularized the concept of online social networking, and from Facebook, the website that perfected it. For the purposes of book marketing, your goal is to populate your "Interesting People & Friends" list with, well, interesting people and friends with whom you share alliances. Hint: These are authors of competitive or similar books.

First, you must create friendships with them. When you do, all their other friends become exposed to you and your book. For anybody who has successfully promoted anything on MySpace, Facebook, or Twitter, you realize how prophetic "Six Degrees of Separation" is. Social networking is a remarkable way to promote a book, a business, and even yourself as an expert in a particular field.

Online friend networking takes the best of multilevel marketing and combines mankind's natural inclination to socialize. How can you leverage this to your advantage? Find authors who have written similar books to yours. Become Amazon Friends with them. Then you will show up in association with them on their Amazon Profile Page. All of a sudden, their marketing efforts are going to increase the amount of exposure you receive.

Some authors of competitive books, or perhaps even random individuals, may take it upon themselves to "fight" against you. Perhaps this is human nature; it certainly is the way competitors have treated each other in the past. But people who do this are missing the point of Amazon, and in the end, only hurting themselves.

If you have done your competitive networking right, so that your book appears on competitive Book Detail Pages while their books appear on yours, these opponents will eventually realize that their disparaging actions are negatively affecting *their* book sales.

Amazon is wonderful that way. It actually promotes and rewards cooperation and goodwill.

★★★★   AUTHOR CENTRAL PROFILE

Before the advent of Author Central, the Amazon Profile Page was much more robust, or, perhaps the proper word is convoluted. Now, Author Central splits the duties so authors have a set of features specifically tailored for the purposes of creating an author webpage and an author community on Amazon.

Once you have signed in to your Author Central account at **amazon.com/authors,** you can update your Author Central profile under the "Profile" tab. Much like your Amazon Profile, here is where you update your biography and your author photo. It is important that both are professional. Your biography should focus on your expertise if you write nonfiction, and your applicable experiences and/or passion if you write fiction. Your biography should avoid mentioning the number of cats you own (unless, of course, you happen to write about cats).

You should also avoid using a photograph of yourself taken by a family member of you standing in front of a wall in your home, or wearing a baseball cap in front of a tree in your backyard. Here is your opportunity to present yourself in a professional light. If you don't take your public persona seriously, no one else will, either.

Have a professional photograph taken, and be sure to acquire the rights from the photographer to use it everywhere. Just because it is a picture of you doesn't mean you automatically own all the rights to it.

Obviously, the simplest method for updating your Author Central account is to duplicate the biography and author photo you used to complete your Author Profile Page.

★★★★   **YOUR AMAZON BLOG**

The Amazon Blog is your online Web journal. You may contribute to it at any time. It is basically an online diary that you update and publish instantly over Amazon for anyone else to read.

The Amazon Blog provides a forum in which to post information about you and your book. You can create (or add to) your blog from the "Blog" tab in your Author Central account. You can also use an RSS feed from another blog you may have elsewhere.

Amazon has jumped on the blog bandwagon. The "Blog" section of Author Central is where you add new postings to your blog and see all your current postings, along with comments that other Amazon visitors have submitted to your blog.

The uses for your blog become more apparent with a thorough review of the Book Detail Page, which occurs in the next chapter. But here is a quick summary:

The Book Detail Page features a description section, which is devoted to editorial reviews, the book's synopsis, author biographies, and sample content for your book. All of this information is somewhat controlled by the distributor and/or publisher of your book. If your book is distributed via Ingram or Baker & Taylor, your distributor or publisher has most likely contributed some preliminary information about your book already. Even if you are providing that information yourself as an independently self-publishing writer, the information is still subject to Amazon review.

The bottom line is that your Book Detail Page may not say some things you want it to say due to publishing procedures or Amazon policies. Your Amazon Blog, on the other hand, offers a forum to say whatever you want in the way of marketing information or supplemental data. You may express your own opinions candidly.

Each posting to your blog is propagated to your Author Page, and each Book Detail Page includes a link to your Author Page. The more books you publish, the more visible your Author Page becomes.

I will reiterate this several times throughout this book, because it's true: *One of the best ways to sell more books on Amazon is to*

One of the best ways to sell more books on Amazon is to publish more books. It takes less than twice the effort to promote two books. It takes far less than three times the effort to promote three books. This is called economy of scale.

publish more books. That may sound obvious, and the obvious reasons are valid. But equally valid is this: It takes less than twice the effort to promote two books. It takes far less than three times the effort to promote three books, and so forth. This is called *economy of scale.* Amazon is weighted heavily in your favor.

Therefore, it is in your best interest to publish multiple books. Sell everything that you have ever written on Amazon. Consult Chapter One again for different methods to publish your books and sell them from Amazon. POD (print-on-demand) technology has made this very easy, quick, and affordable.

Depending upon the settings you use for your blog, Amazon users can comment on your blog postings. Their comments are also available for public perusal and rebuttal. By responding to a comment made on your blog you create a public dialogue, which becomes indexed by search engines. I highly recommend this. The easiest way to add blog content is to encourage other people to write the content for you. All you need to do is respond positively. This is not the place to wage a verbal war with someone. Always be positive, informed, and upbeat. Remember, your words are constantly judged by others who are considering your book for purchase.

There are additional advantages to sharing blog comments with others, particularly if you are in the same category as a famous author with whom you can create a rapport.

For example, a back-and-forth communication between you and Stephanie Meyer would be very valuable for you if you also happen to write romantic vampire books. Other fans who are reading Stephanie Meyer's blog may read your responses (all of which include your Personal Headline, which mentions your book of course). More exposure means more clicks either to your Amazon Profile or your Author Page. If both are complete and professional, that translates to more clicks to your book.

In that light, it is also important to make an effort to comment on other people's blogs, particularly those in your network of similar and competitive books. More comments from you means more exposure, which means more clicks to your Amazon Profile and Author Page, etc.

Since your blog content appears on your Author Page and since links to your Author Page appear on your Book Detail Page, consider using your blog to control the information available to the public about your book.

It is also important to make an effort to comment on other people's blogs, particularly those in your network of similar and competitive books.

Also be sure to take full advantage of the capabilities of blogs by adding links, images, and video. A recent Internet report indicates that 40% of all Internet usage revolves around online video. Web surfers like videos first, images second, links third, and plain text least of all. Ironically, this means that as a writer, you should use words as infrequently as possible to sell your writing. Fortunately, blogs make that somewhat easy to accomplish.

★★★★   ## YOUR BIBLIOGRAPHY

Bibliographies list books on a particular topic or written by a particular author. In Amazon's case, that author is you. Amazon only cares about your books if they are available for sale on Amazon. If you have written other books that are not on Amazon yet, Amazon will not add those books to your bibliography. In that case, your first order of business involves publishing and listing all your books.

Remember what I said a few pages ago? Publish everything you have written. List everything you have published on Amazon. Use your Author Page to link everything together. After all, the effort you are expending for one book easily promotes two. Amazon makes it simple to leverage your techniques through online propagation of data, which makes it easy and fast to promote multiple books simultaneously.

Leveraging your marketing initiatives is more efficient for you and for your pocket-book because the effort is nearly the same and the results are twofold or even three-fold. The goal is to make that effort multiply itself by the number of books you have published.

I mentioned *economy of scale* earlier; *leverage* is its cousin. Leverage is the foundation upon which wealth is built. Simply put, leverage enables you to do more with less. Leverage creates maximum results with minimum effort. More book sales with less book marketing.

Let us look specifically at my bibliography. At the time of this writing, I have eight books listed. I have a children's book titled *Aidan's Shoes* and four books about publishing, three of which have both paperback and Kindle editions: *Self-Publishing Simplified, Publishing Gems,* and *Sell Your Book on Amazon.*

The lone Kindle holdout in my publishing genre is *Adventures in Publishing.* It features full-color illustrations and is therefore not appropriate for the Kindle.

> Leverage is the foundation upon which wealth is built. Simply put, leverage enables you to do more with less. Leverage creates maximum results with minimum effort.

Based upon my bibliography, you may be able to tell that I recommend Kindle editions for all black-and-white books. I will discuss the Kindle in more detail later.

The point is, my promotion efforts for *Sell Your Book on Amazon* result in book sales for my other books (and vice versa). Efforts directed toward the promotion of one book are resulting in the sale of multiple books. That's leverage.

Amazon requires verification of your bibliography. This means a third party, typically the publisher, must verify your status as the author. The process of creating and maintaining your bibliography starts on the "Books" tab of your Author Central Page.

CHAPTER 3

THE BOOK DETAIL PAGE

The single most important Amazon page for authors is the page that showcases their book. The Sales Page, or Book Detail Page, has all the information a consumer will need to make a purchasing decision. It is the page on Amazon that exists solely for the purpose of informing people about your book and selling copies of your book.

Understanding and systematically building your Book Detail Page is a very important part of your success on Amazon. So we are going to discuss all the elements comprehensively.

For the purposes of this chapter, I will refer to the Book Detail Page that features one of my books, titled *Self-Publishing Simplified*. I hope you have the opportunity to review this chapter in front of a computer because your overall learning will be enhanced by viewing my Book Detail Page along with me. Then, once you are comfortable, transition to the Book Detail Page for your book. There will be differences. The look and feel of each Book Detail Page is largely dependent upon the information the author and/or publisher supplies to Amazon about the book.

The advantage to viewing my example first is that all the elements I cover in this chapter are there. In all likelihood the Book

Fig. 3 - www.amazon.com/dp/1598000810

Detail Page for your book looks substantially different and may not be as beneficial to the learning process. Of course, my Book Detail Page may have changed somewhat since this screenshot was taken, too. That is the advantage of online information and the disadvantage of paper books.

Amazon presents webpages dynamically to the user based upon the user's preferences. In other words, Amazon remembers what products a user purchases and what products a user expresses interest in and then creates a personal shopping experience accordingly.

What does that mean? Even if you are looking at the Book Detail Page for *Self-Publishing Simplified*, your experience may differ from what I describe because Amazon displays information pertaining to other products you have viewed previously. My specific book data is consistent, but some supplementary product information varies by viewer. It is this unique experience that defines Amazon. It is what makes Amazon so important to understand when you are trying to sell your book. That dynamic experience means Amazon is tailoring your experience to your wants and desires. Amazon tries to anticipate what products you want. The more information Amazon has about you and your book, the more likely it is that Amazon will

Amazon presents webpages dynamically to the user based upon the user's preferences. In other words, Amazon creates a personal shopping experiences based upon products you have bought in the past.

find other shoppers interested in your book. Subsequently, Amazon uses that knowledge to tailor a unique experience for all its shoppers, which may include introducing your book to new buyers.

You can view the Book Detail Page for my book by first searching for *Self-Publishing Simplified* in the Amazon search box. My book will appear on the results list. Click on the title or cover image so we can examine the Book Detail Page from top to bottom.

★★★★★   SEARCH INSIDE

The most noticeable element of any Book Detail Page is the cover image. Amazon knows that people judge books by their covers, so the cover image is placed conspicuously in the upper left portion of the page. The Search Inside graphic is above the cover graphic and says "Click to Look Inside." For the sake of brevity, I will simply call it Search Inside.

When you go into a bookstore and pick up a book, you can flip it over in your hands, fan the pages, and read the first paragraph. Search Inside is Amazon's answer to browsing books at an actual bookstore; it enables you to scan through a select number of digital pages of the book. It is Amazon's hope that this functionality entices more customers to purchase the book. If Amazon is to be believed, it does. They claim that books participating in Search Inside sell better than books that do not participate.

That fact alone should convince you to participate in Search Inside. But if not, here is another reason: Participating in Search Inside digitizes your book and makes it available for Amazon's computer to dissect and analyze. By scanning and storing the entire contents of your book, Amazon extracts additional information other than just the title, author name, and ISBN. Therefore, it is more likely that Amazon's search engine will present your book in search results to people who enter applicable search terms.

The more information Amazon has about your book, the more exposure your book receives. If there is one overall theme to this book, it is about increasing your exposure and your book's exposure on Amazon.

As the author, you are already aware of your book and its Book Detail Page. You may look at it all the time, but you probably never intend to buy your own book. The trick, therefore, is to get people who have never heard of you or your book to discover it themselves. They need to learn about it through the unique shopping experiences Amazon

> Search Inside digitizes your book and makes it available to dissect and analyze. By scanning and storing the contents, Amazon extracts information in addition to the title, author name, and ISBN.

There is controversy about Search Inside's contractual terms. Once clause in the contract gives Amazon the right to hold the digital data for your title indefinitely.

creates for them. In order for that to happen, Amazon needs a lot of information about your book.

I recommend Search Inside for all books. There is controversy about the program, particularly in terms of its contractual language. A certain clause in the contract gives Amazon the right to hold the digital data for your title indefinitely. Even if Amazon no longer has the right to sell your book anymore, they still have the right to display the book on their website, albeit it "out of stock" or "out of print."

That contractual clause concerns some publishers and authors who dislike the notion of granting any perpetual rights, digital or otherwise. Do not hold this against me, but in my personal experience, I have not seen any downside. Amazon is in business to make money by helping authors, not stealing from them.

Ultimately, the Search Inside the Book program helps Amazon duplicate a bookstore experience. Right now, the Internet has not found a way to replicate fully that three-dimensional experience any other way. Until it does, Search Inside is Amazon's answer. Visit **www.amazon.com/sitb** if you want to sign up for Search Inside. Amazon will need an unsecured PDF file from you.

TITLE INFORMATION

To the right of the Search Inside logo and cover image is the title and subtitle of the book. Your title and subtitle combination should contain every conceivable search phrase you can think of regarding your topic.

Next to the title, in parentheses, is the binding type, and underneath the title is the byline or author's name. By clicking on the byline, one of two things happens. If you have only one book on Amazon, the search results show similar author matches. If you have multiple books on Amazon, a "pop-up" with related author links appears, including a way to access the author's Amazon webpage.

I recommend against doing what I originally did as the author of *Self-Publishing Simplified* (I used my company name as the author) because Amazon did not display my full bibliography when clicking my byline. I since changed it, and now buyers see all the other books I have written, including the one in your hand. When the author was listed as "Outskirtspress.com" instead of "Brent Sampson," Amazon did not recognize my other publications and therefore did not promote them through my *Self-Publishing Simplified* byline.

One of the requirements of successfully branding yourself as a writer is publishing multiple books. If you have written multiple books, the author link immediately increases the exposure of all your books. Not only is that a branding element all in itself, it is also a way of marketing to a pre-qualified buyer. If consumers read a book by you and want to read others, Amazon makes it easy for them to find all your books.

If you are exerting effort to promote one book, and Amazon makes it this easy to cross-promote two, you might as well publish more books, right? Only have one book so far? Get busy. The efficiencies multiply as you publish more books on Amazon.

Next to the byline, Amazon displays "key phrases" from the book, provided the book has been submitted to the Search Inside the Book program.

In the case of my book, Amazon displays key phrases like *laminated hardback* and *standard digital distribution*, among others. If you click on one of the key phrases, Amazon takes you to a listing of other books that feature the same key phrase. Why is this important? Because it lets you identify similar titles in your competitive network. You will soon recognize the need for that if you don't already.

> If consumers read a book by you and want to read others, Amazon makes it easy for them to find all your books.

Underneath "Key Phrases" is the average review rank and the number of reviews that have been composed. By clicking on the link, the Book Detail Page displays all the reviews in reverse chronological order, with the most recent ones appearing first. We will discuss reviews later in this chapter.

LIST PRICE

Underneath the average review rank is "List Price," which is synonymous with the suggested retail price of the book. If the book is discounted, a secondary number, called "Price," is directly below "List Price."

Amazon (not the author or publisher) decides which books to discount based upon a number of factors, including the season, the publisher, and most importantly, Amazon's profit margin on the book.

In the case of *Self-Publishing Simplified*, I expect Amazon always to sell it for the list price—that is, without any discounting. I wanted to make this book as inexpensive as possible to encourage maximum readership. As a result, there is basically zero margin for Amazon to discount the price further. I discuss pricing options in Chapter Seven.

Fortunately, *Self-Publishing Simplified* is eligible for Amazon's own Free Super Saver Shipping promotion. Bonus promotions such as this are reasons your marketing efforts should direct book sales through Amazon. Perhaps a user decides to buy your book for no other reason than to qualify for Super Saver Shipping. A sale is a sale, and Amazon is a slick salesperson... er, computer.

★★★   **AMAZON MARKETPLACE**

Below the pricing of the book is its availability. This section also reports the anticipated wait time for delivery or fulfillment.

Time for another controversial section of Amazon—the Marketplace. Below "Availability" is a line of text claiming that multiple copies of the book are available in both "new" and "used" conditions for drastically reduced prices.

How can Amazon sell books cheaper than its own discounted price? What does this mean? It means that Amazon is both a retail store and a yard sale. Clicking on either the **new** or **used** link brings up the Marketplace listings for that book.

At one time, there actually used to be a little heading for this link that called itself the

"Marketplace" section. Perhaps Amazon is still struggling with how to deal with this section, because there is some confusion about it. Hence, the controversy.

On one level, Marketplace is similar to eBay. Individuals sell copies of the featured book in a variety of conditions ranging from "New" to "Collectible."

On another level, Marketplace is like eBay Shops, where businesses use Amazon Marketplace as a forum to showcase *all* their wares. In this case, most of the businesses may not even have the book in stock. If a book is distributed by a wholesaler like Ingram, individuals or companies within the "Marketplace" section often respond to an order just as a bookstore would—they order the book after it is requested.

In the case of print-on-demand books, these vendors are listing books exactly the way Amazon does—by displaying the data of the book, often without having the physical book in inventory.

To understand that concept more clearly, it is important to understand how print-on-demand works. In some ways, print-on-demand inventory is similar to money within a bank account. When you see $1,000 in your account, it does not mean your local bank has one thousand crisp one-dollar bills in a personal

Amazon Marketplace is similar to eBay. Individuals sell copies of the featured book in a variety of conditions ranging from New to Collectible.

In the case of Marketplace listings, many individuals and companies do not have the actual book. If a book is print-on-demand, the book might not even be printed yet.

vault with your name on it. Rather, the bank represents your money electronically. When you visit the bank and request your money, they get it for you. But the amount of physical cash the bank has on hand is lower than the amount of money they represent to all their customers electronically.

Print-on-demand book inventory is similar. A book is represented electronically. When the demand is made, the book is printed and delivered. If *all* the on-demand authors demanded copies of their books at the same time, demand would exceed capacity, just as it did for banks during the Great Depression when an inordinate number of people demanded their money simultaneously.

In the case of Marketplace listings, many of the individuals and companies (let's call them vendors) do not have the actual book. If a book is print-on-demand, the book might not even be printed yet.

If you were to request or purchase the book from one of these Marketplace vendors, they would turn around and purchase it through the publisher or wholesaler. They may even buy it from Amazon themselves. It is a common tactic. Amazon itself often does not have copies of the books it sells until after they have been ordered. Their warehouse simply isn't *that* big.

Many Marketplace vendors are savvy businesspeople. They use Amazon as a forum in which to promote their companies. Amazon Marketplace provides a cost-effective way to publicize their bookstores or services to the world market.

Describing the condition of a book is where savvy Marketplace vendors take advantage of Amazon. They use all nine condition choices to multiply the amount of listings their company receives in the Marketplace results. If a Marketplace vendor has multiple copies of your book, but all of them are indicated as new, then that vendor is going to appear in the "Marketplace" section only once. However, Marketplace vendors who indicate other conditions for the same book appear in the Marketplace listings multiple times, once for each condition of the book.

So you may see many vendors selling many copies of your book in many different conditions, which explains why the Amazon Book Detail Page reports "22 new" and "14 used" copies of your book, for example. Marketplace vendors indicate different conditions for the book based on nothing more than their desire to have multiple listings in the "Marketplace" section.

Just understanding how Amazon Marketplace works typically addresses the most com-

> Marketplace vendors are savvy businesspeople. They use Amazon as a forum in which to promote their companies and publicize their services to the world market.

mon concerns about it. And understanding is half the battle. The other half is action. Yes, you can use Marketplace to your advantage.

★★★   **MARKETPLACE SUBMISSIONS**

You may choose to use Amazon's Marketplace to sell copies of your book that you own as the legitimate author. If you have published your book independently, you may have thousands of books sitting in your garage where your car should be, and you may be wondering how to sell some. Amazon Marketplace offers one solution. If you have an exclusive distributor or wholesale relationships, check with them first; but they should be okay with you listing some copies of your book through Amazon Marketplace.

Keep in mind you need to fulfill Marketplace orders yourself. This differs from standard Amazon listings, where nearly all mainstream publishers and on-demand publishers handle Amazon order fulfillment for you.

If you are wondering how you can sell signed copies of your book on Amazon without having to pay 55% through Amazon Advantage, the answer is Amazon Marketplace.

To the far right of the Book Detail Page, underneath the "Add to Shopping Cart" box is a secondary box with the caption, "More Buying Choices." At the base of that box is a button that says **Sell Yours Here**. Clicking on that button displays the submission screen for Amazon Marketplace. Amazon will ask you to confirm the book you want to sell.

Then Amazon asks you to select the condition of your item. You have nine choices ranging from "New" to "Collectible-Accept-

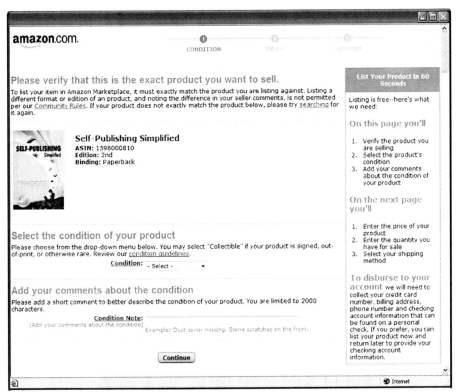

Fig. 4 - www.amazon.com/marketplace

able." A collectible could be a signed edition, or maybe it is from the first print run. Demonstrating that the book is special will help you differentiate it from other Marketplace listings. Use the "Add your comments about the condition" section to indicate whether your book is a signed copy, for example.

★★★★★   **SHARE WITH FRIENDS**

Let us return to the Book Detail Page and stay on the far right of the screen, where there are a variety of other buttons for functions such as "Wish List" and "Free 2-day Shipping," among others. These buttons hold very little in the way of promotional opportunity, so we'll skip them.

However, the last link on that right column, **Share with Friends,** is useful. You have probably seen this functionality on websites before. It enables you to send an email to someone you know, notifying them about the website you are visiting.

Talk about a webpage that you have justification to share with others—the Book Detail Page on Amazon featuring your very own published book! Not only have you published a book, but it is available worldwide on Amazon.com, the world-renowned bookstore. This really is something to promote. A published book lends credibility and helps establish expertise status.

Open your Rolodex or look in your email address book. Send an email to everybody you know with an email address. This isn't spam; you are informing other associates, colleagues, business partners, friends, family, and neighbors of your published book on Amazon. You *should* be proud.

Even better, since you are using Amazon's functionality, your message is sent through their email server. It looks like an official Amazon offer (because it is one), but also features a personal message you can compose in advance.

Once you have identified your recipients and composed your outgoing message, Amazon creates an email that displays the cover of your book and lets your recipients click on a link to access your Book Detail Page immediately.

All of Amazon's tools share the same objective—making it easy for people to find and buy products on Amazon. The "Share with Friends" function is the easiest possible way for people you know to find your book and buy it. Each time you get a new contact, use this function to tell them about your book.

Not only have you published a book, but it is available worldwide on Amazon.com. A published book lends credibility and helps establish expertise status.

★★★   ADDITIONAL IMAGE VIEWS

We are going to jump over to the left of the screen now. Underneath the *Self-Publishing Simplified* cover are little thumbnail images. Put your mouse over each one and the cover image changes to a larger view of the thumbnail image.

For the most part, additional images are somewhat superfluous. However, if you have a book that heavily features images, such as children's books or art books, adding these images to your Book Detail Page can only help. Chapter Six discusses how.

★★★★★   FREQUENTLY BOUGHT TOGETHER

The first major section to concentrate on is called "Frequently Bought Together." If your book does not have this section, then your first step is acquiring one. This is accomplished by selling a number of books on Amazon, so that Amazon's algorithm recognizes the buying patterns of your customers.

Until 2009, this section was titled either "Better Together" or "Best Value," depending upon what promotional efforts the author or publisher were taking. Amazon offered a co-op advertising program known as the BXGY promotion ("buy x, get y"), whereby one could pay to have a book "paired" with a higher-ranked book. It was also known as the Paid Placement program. In 2009, Amazon stopped offering the BXGY promotion publicly.

Participating in the BXGY promotion was the easiest, most expensive way to get your book paired with a higher-ranked book and receive an almost immediate improvement to your sales rank. In fact, if you participated in the program long enough, Amazon's engine would start to pair your book with the higher-ranked book even if you *didn't* pay for it.

Even though Amazon has discontinued the BXGY promotion, I discuss it in further detail in Chapter Six, partly because I believe Amazon may reintroduce the program sometime in the future. It was a cash cow for Amazon, although not often cost-effective for individual authors.

Once Amazon has enough information about your book's customers to create a "Frequently Bought Together" section, it will appear on your Book Detail Page through no effort on your part. This section shows a pair of related books, ostensibly for the purpose of encouraging multiple-book purchases.

Participating in the BXGY promotion was the easiest way to get your book paired with a higher-ranked book and receive an improvement to your rank.

Your goal is to make your book one of the books Amazon selects to include on *other* Book Detail Pages. For example, *Sell Your Book on Amazon* is often paired with *Self-Publishing Simplified* because Amazon has evidence demonstrating that the same shoppers buy both. The effort I put forth promoting *Self-Publishing Simplified* is resulting in additional exposure for *Sell Your Book on Amazon*.

The point is that *Sell Your Book on Amazon* receives extra exposure (and sales) due to the marketing efforts I put forth promoting *Self-Publishing Simplified* (and vice-versa), and that cross-promotional benefit is due largely to this section.

By the same token, the effort other authors put forth promoting their books will result in additional exposure for your book if your book is in their "Frequently Bought Together" sections.

For example, *Sell Your Book on Amazon* appears in the "Frequently Bought Together" section on many other highly-ranked Detail Pages, including Dan Poynter's *The Self-Publishing Manual*. A combination of many tactics detailed in this book is what got it there; it is an excellent position to be in and a goal you want to shoot for with your book.

PRODUCT PROMOTIONS

Directly below the "Frequently Bought Together" section is the "Special Offers and Product Promotions" section. Here Amazon lists the promotions available for your book.

Over 100,000 books are eligible for the 4-for-3 promotion. This special offer for *Self-Publishing Simplified* appeared automatically on my Book Detail Page shortly after I submitted my book to the Search Inside program. It makes my book eligible for a promotion through no effort of my own.

If you are looking for reasons to market and sell your book on Amazon, this is one. No other website on earth matches the merchandising capability of Amazon. Is another website going to offer incentives like free shipping for purchases in excess of $25 and/or 4-for-3 promotions that encourage additional purchases? Maybe. But is another website also going to remember every action each consumer takes and tailor that consumer's experience in an effort to introduce them to new products? No.

That is exactly what Amazon does. If you buy a cookbook on Amazon, your very next visit to Amazon may include suggestions for other cookbooks. The authors of those other cookbooks benefit from Amazon's algorithm, because their books are being displayed to you solely because you bought a similar book.

So, this 4-for-3 promotion is just another tactic Amazon takes to encourage people to buy your book. It does not affect your discount or your royalty. But it does help close sales, which is what Amazon does better than any other book retailer. I don't give this tactic a "star rating" because this isn't something you have control over; Amazon decides which books receive promotions.

★★★★★   ## CUSTOMERS WHO BOUGHT...

Directly below "Special Offers and Product Promotions" is a section with a heading that reads, "Customers Who Bought This Item Also Bought." You will see up to seven books related to yours along with buttons to scroll left or right for even more book suggestions.

This section helps you determine your audience based upon their buying habits. While you may not necessarily receive a demographic analysis, you can extract anecdotal information to help you market your book more successfully.

For example, customers who bought *Self-Publishing Simplified* also bought *Sell Your Book on Amazon*, *The Self-Publishing Manual*, *The Complete Guide to Self Publishing*, *The Complete Idiot's Guide to Self-Publishing*, and *Top Self-Publishing Firms*, among others.

In other words, this section tells me which books I should consider reading and writing reviews for. This also tells me what books I should consider including on my Listmania Lists and Amazon Guides, both of which are discussed at length in Chapters Four and Five, respectively.

Simply put, this is the list of the books in your competitive network. Make a note of all these books and look at the Book Detail Pages for all of them. Consider purchasing many of them so you can further establish your expertise in your field, and so you can write reviews for each of them.

Ultimately, it matters not that these books appear in the "Customers Who Bought This Item Also Bought" section on your Book Detail Page. What matters is whether you are successful at getting your book in this section on *their* Book Detail Page. The more Book Detail Pages your book appears on, the more books you are going to sell, and *that's* the goal that earns this tactic a five-star rating.

> The more Book Detail Pages your book appears on, the more books you are going to sell.

★★★★★   **EDITORIAL REVIEWS**

The "Editorial Reviews" section is the synopsis area for your book. Here is where you see the description of the book supplied by the distributor, wholesaler, or publisher. You may also see trade magazine or journal reviews. This section can be fairly comprehensive, including an author biography, a sample chapter, a table of contents for the entire book, and even a personal note from both the author and the publisher.

If information is missing, you can add it. I discuss the way to add editorial content within Chapter Six, but basically, you complete a form on Amazon's website at: **www.amazon.com/add-content-books**

You can submit book information, editorial reviews, peer reviews from the publisher, and so on.

Because of the extent of information sometimes available in the "Editorial Reviews" section, it is not uncommon for Amazon to condense the section into a smaller snapshot, highlighting just the description or just two reviews. That is why there is sometimes a link that says, **See all editorial reviews**. This is not ideal because it will appear as if your book has *less* information at first glance, and it is unlikely that

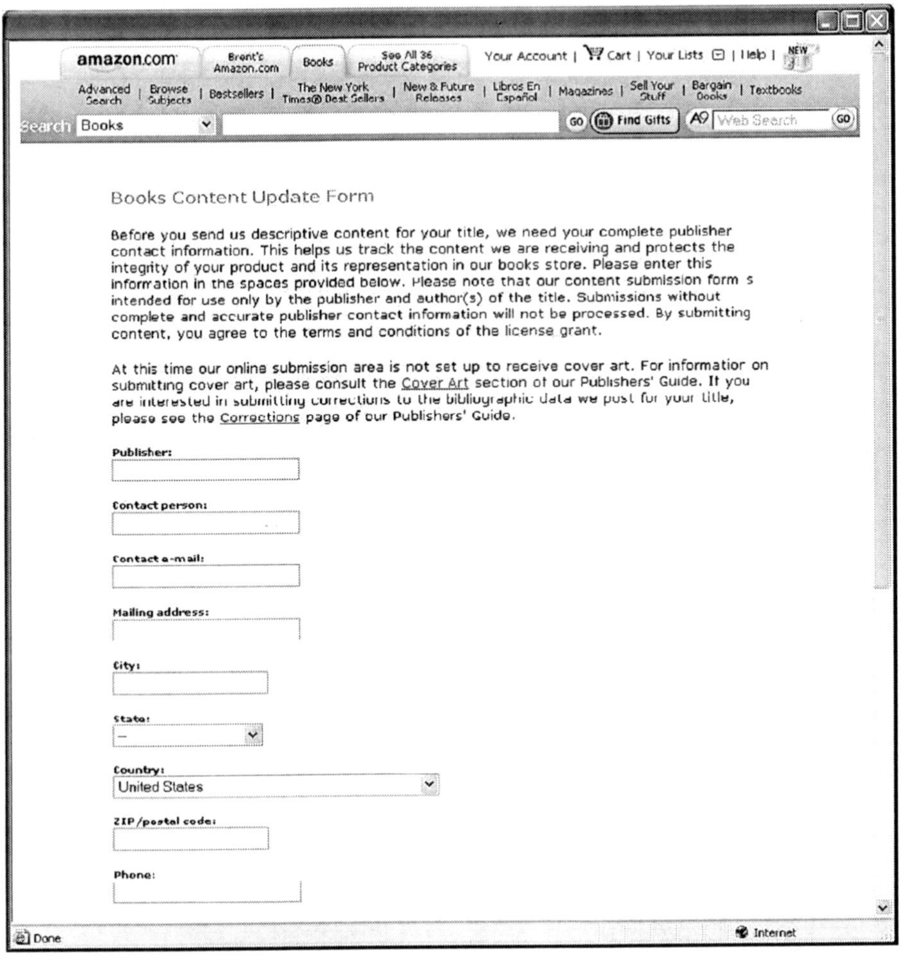

Fig. 5 - www.amazon.com/add-content-books

people will click on that link to see all the details. Avoid this by placing all your content within the first section of the form.

Ideally, your "Editorial Reviews" section should contain between 3,500 and 4,000 characters of content. The more comprehensive your "Editorial Reviews" section is, the more books you are going to sell.

Remember, since customers cannot touch your physical book and flip through the pages, it is important to use this section to give them as much information about the book as possible.

PRODUCT DETAILS

Next on the Book Detail Page comes the "Product Details" section, in which certain specifications about the book are displayed, including:

- format
- page count
- publisher
- publication date
- language
- ISBN

Also within this section you will see the average customer review, the number of reviews the book has received, and a link to compose a review. We will discuss reviews later in this chapter.

Also shown is the Amazon sales rank. Let us take this opportunity to dispel the mystery surrounding the Amazon sales rank.

AMAZON SALES RANK

Since the algorithm Amazon uses to generate a book's sales rank is proprietary, details can only be extrapolated from research and field tests. Suffice it to say the Amazon sales rank provides marginal sales data at best. Ultimately, it provides only anecdotal information about your book's sales performance.

Your rank is in no way an exact sales figure. Having an Amazon sales rank of 288,166 does not mean you have sold 288,166 copies of your book. In fact, the opposite is closer to the truth. The higher the rank number, the lower your book sales.

Amazon's own perspective on the sales rank and its importance can be discerned from Amazon's online FAQ that states (slightly paraphrased): "The Sales Ranking system exhibits how books are selling. The lower the number, the higher the sales. The calculation is based on sales and is updated each hour to reflect recent and historical sales of every item sold. We hope you find the Amazon.com Sales Rank interesting!"

Please notice that you are not supposed to find the sales rank informative or even helpful. You are supposed to find it interesting.

The Sales Ranking system exhibits how books are selling. The lower the number, the higher the sales. The calculation is based on sales and is updated each hour.

In actuality, the process *is* interesting and is more convoluted than their FAQ reveals. The rankings are updated every hour and do not depend solely upon the actual number of books sold, but also upon comparisons against the sales trends of other books during that same hour. Simultaneously, a trending calculation is applied to arrive at a computerized sales trajectory.

Trending projections and historic sales information play a key role in determining the rank for titles in the 10,000 to 100,000 range. In fact, the predictive nature of the Amazon ranking system is what makes it possible for a newly released book to outrank an older, more-established title, even though the total historic sales figures for the latter far exceed the former.

Books with rankings over 100,000 are also applied with historic sales information and projections, although sales history is weighted less. Sales projections and trending take an active role for books in this range, which is why a book's rank can leap from 900,000 to 100,000 in the span of twenty-four hours or less. Does this mean the book has sold 800,000 copies in twenty-four hours? Absolutely not! What it does mean is that recent activity (i.e., purchases) for that book is trending higher than all the books it just surpassed in that particular hour. Don't get excited just yet. Since the activity of books above 100,000 ranges from slow to stagnant, receiving as few as five orders is sufficient to catapult a rank.

If a book's rank breaks into the top 100,000, the sales history calculation starts in earnest, which is why a phenomenon book has a hard time maintaining a high, legitimate ranking. A *phenomenon book* is a book that leaps from the high hundred thousands into the lower hundreds (or better) in the span of twenty-four hours, usually due to some concentrated marketing initiatives. Since Amazon's sales history does not support the rank, the spike occurs and then quickly levels out again to display a more accurate ranking.

It is impossible to use Amazon's sales rank to calculate cumulative sales figures because the data is recalculated continually. To get a rough idea of the actual number of books being sold, a book's rank has to be dissected with the same immediacy as the ranking being calculated. For instance, chart the rank of a top 10,000 book every hour for twenty-four hours. Add those rankings together and divide by twenty-four to arrive at its average daily ranking. Do that every day for a week and then divide by seven to arrive at its average weekly ranking.

Since the activity of books above 100,000 ranges from slow to stagnant, receiving as few as five orders is sufficient to catapult a rank.

With that average sales rank in hand, you are prepared to estimate the sales potential of the book using the following chart.

Bear in mind that this chart is extremely arbitrary, based upon sales rank and sales-figure comparisons along with data (both confirmed and not confirmed) received from third-party sources.

Rather than disclaiming this chart until the cows come home, I will just say this: It is difficult to extract meaningful information from data that isn't very meaningful. But it sure is interesting, and now, perhaps, even slightly helpful.

Av. Ranking	Book Sales Potential
2,000,000+	A single consignment copy has sold
1,000,000+	Total sales may not exceed 50
100,000+	Total sales may not exceed 200
10,000+	Estimate 1–50 copies sold per week
1,000+	Estimate 10–100 copies sold per week
100+	Estimate 1–100 copies sold per day
10+	Estimate 100–500 copies sold per day
Under 10	Up to and over 500 copies sold per day

Next to the Amazon sales rank on the Book Detail Page is a link to **See Bestsellers in Books.** This is an easy way to see the top-selling books on Amazon at any given time. It is updated hourly and is your source for picking books to complement your Listmania Lists and Amazon Guides.

Obviously, the more popular a book is, the more valuable it is to your marketing efforts. The best-case scenario is when you discover a highly ranked book that is also part of your competitive network. In those cases, do all you can to associate your book with that highly ranked competitive book immediately. Read the book, write a positive review for it, create a Listmania List and Guide for it, etc.

Below the Amazon sales rank, in a smaller font, you will see a link that says, "What's this?" And here you will learn the difference between an Amazon sales rank and a category sales rank. For instance, depending upon your category niche, you might be ranked #1 in a certain category, but ranked in the millions on Amazon overall.

The last link in the "Product Details" section enables you to **update product info** and **give feedback on images**. The former is particularly helpful if you want to personally notify Amazon of an error on the Book Detail Page. For instance, you may wish to update the title, author, binding, publication date, publisher, number of pages, edition, format, or language. Since computers are often responsible for providing the majority of this information to Amazon, it is valuable to have an easy way to correct data.

> The more popular a book is, the more valuable it is to your marketing efforts. The best-case scenario is when you discover a highly ranked book that is also part of your competitive network.

★★★★   MORE ABOUT THE AUTHOR

The next section on the Book Detail Page is the "More About the Author" section.

Unless you have signed up for an Author Central account, you are not going to have this section on your page. See Chapter Two for more information about creating your Author Central account and completing your Profile.

My "More About the Author" section features a picture of me along with a link to my Amazon Author Page. Since Amazon makes it so easy to visit Author Pages, you want your Author Page to be professional. One of the main goals of *Sell Your Book on Amazon* is to help you increase your exposure on Amazon and demonstrate to other people that you are the expert in whatever field you are writing about. People buy books from experts.

So, if you are an expert in publishing, you want your Author Page to establish that; and if you have published multiple books on the subject, you want your bibliography to communicate that, too.

Selling a book is all a matter of repetition. When Amazon shoppers constantly see your picture, read your book synopsis, or see the cover of your book, they start to perceive activity surrounding your book. Exposure builds upon itself and consumers think, "Gosh, I had better buy this book. I don't want to be left behind."

That feeling then encourages them to visit your Book Detail Page and find out all about you and your book. Since people typically purchase nonfiction books based upon the answers to two questions, the information on your Book Detail Page should answer both:

- Will this book help me solve my problem?
- Is this author qualified to offer helpful advice?

The majority of the Book Detail Page is devoted to answering the first question. Therefore, your Author Page and Amazon Profile must answer the second question.

For example, my Amazon Author Page features my Amazon Blog. One of the nice things about creating a blog on Amazon is that you can set it up to automatically repeat blog postings originating elsewhere. I have a blog at **www.brentsampson.com** that is hosted by WordPress. Therefore, thanks to the magic of RSS, every blog posting I write automatically appears on my Amazon Author Page, too. Setting this automation up is remarkably easy. Simply click on the "Blog" tab within your Author Central account, and then enter in your RSS feed into the box. Your blogging platform can provide your specific feed URL.

Blogging is a powerful marketing tool if you use it correctly. You can add additional content like articles or graphs, or you can touch base with the people reading your page and invite their feedback. Other people can post comments to your postings and you can post replies to their comments.

Fig. 6 - Amazon Author Page

A huge benefit to adding your blog to your Author Page is that you control exactly what it says. Amazon is far more lenient about blog content and enforces less censorship than with other areas of your Book Detail Page. So while you are unable to link to a domain name within many fields on the Detail Page, you can link to external websites from your blog.

Yes, you can actually create hyperlinks within your blog postings. Now, all of a sudden, you have a hyperlink from Amazon. com to your author website or directly to your other books on Amazon, or even to your own company—and how powerful of a marketing tool is that?

INSIDE THIS BOOK

The next section of the Book Detail Page is the "Inside This Book" section. I mentioned the Search Inside the Book program briefly at the beginning of this chapter and I will discuss it in greater detail now.

The data available within this section is fascinating, although not necessarily from a promotional point of view. Only after submitting your book to the Search Inside the Book program will this section be displayed.

Some information is displayed only if you are the author of the book. For example, when viewing *Self-Publishing Simplified's* Book Detail Page, a visitor is able only to browse sample pages and search inside the book. On the other hand, as the author of *Self-Publishing Simplified*, Amazon presents me with a robust analysis of my content that lets me study how I write in relation to other books in my category.

Once you submit your book to Search Inside, you will receive this same degree of analysis for your book. You can view key phrases and statistically improbable phrases. A statistically improbable phrase, or SIP, is a phrase or collection of words that are not necessarily related to one another and yet occur frequently together within your book. For example, *Self-Publishing Simplified* contains statistically improbable phrases like *laminated hardback* and *standard digital distribution*.

After submitting your book to the Search Inside program, Amazon provides a robust analysis of your content that lets you study your craft in relation to other books in your category.

You will probably never see the words "standard digital distribution" within *Harry Potter and the Deathly Hallows,* and yet that phrase occurs frequently in *Self-Publishing Simplified*.

How does this help you? It enables you to look for other books that share statistically improbable phrases so that you can locate books within your competitive network.

Your competitive network is the collection of similar books and their authors. You want to associate your Book Detail Page with every similar book and author you find. One way to locate them is through the examination and analysis of your statistically improbable phrases.

Keep in mind that most of the information available within the "Inside This Book" section is meant for the author of the book. So your experience with this section will be vastly different for *your* book than it will be for *Self-Publishing Simplified*. To that end, I will mention another link within this section that is available only for the author: **Books on Related Topics.**

When you click that link, Amazon displays a collection of books that cover related subjects. The books that appear are prime candidates for your network of similar books.

Below your list of books on related topics is your concordance, which displays the one hundred most frequently used words in your book. The words are alphabetized and the font size indicates the relative number of occurrences. The concordance holds little promotional value but is interesting from a writer's perspective, nonetheless.

In the same vein are the "Text Stats" that appear below the concordance. Your

> You want to associate your book with every similar book you find. One way to locate similar books is by matching statistically improbable phrases.

"Text Stats" are divided into subsections: readability, complexity, number of words, and fun stats.

The *readability index* is a graphic representation of the ease with which readers will understand your book in relation to other books. Comparing your book against all other books on Amazon is mostly pointless, but you may also compare your book exclusively against other books in your category. This exercise may help you understand how appropriately your book is composed for your audience. While this may not be beneficial for the promotion of your current book,

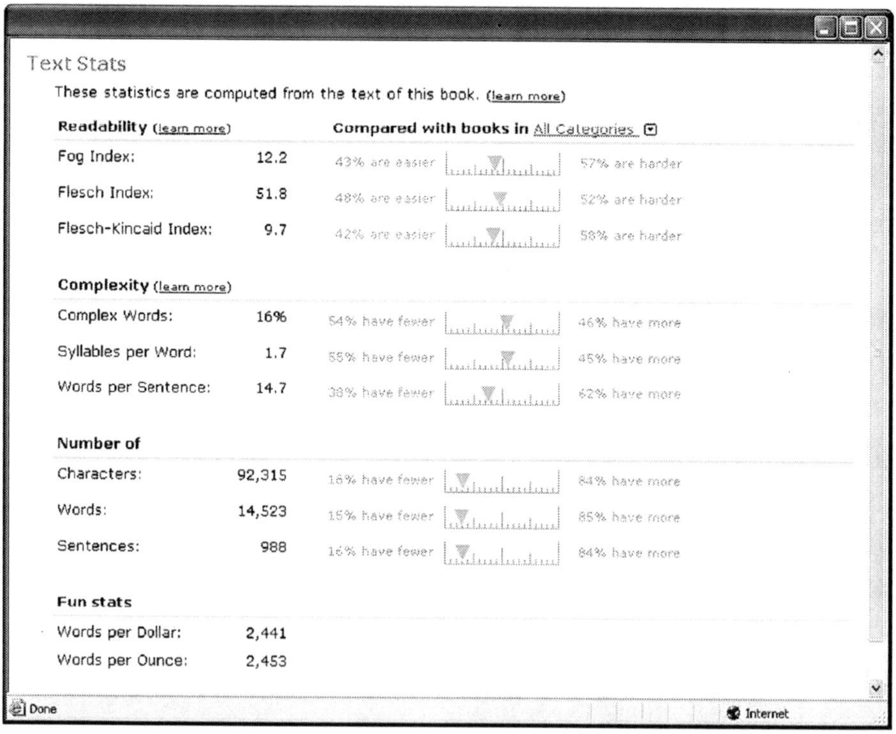

Fig. 7 - Text Statistics

it could prove to be a boon when drafting your next book.

The additional statistics also provide the same level of *edutainment*.

Return to the main Book Detail Page and let us complete the "Inside This Book" section by discussing the "Search Inside This Book" box.

This Amazon functionality lets you search within the content of the book, provided the book has been submitted to the Search Inside the Book program. Searching the content of a book is advantageous because people may not necessarily know the title of a book or the name of the author, but they know the subjects that interest them. Only by submitting your book to the Search Inside the Book program does Amazon have enough information to present contextual search results. This search box lets readers determine if your book is truly what they are seeking.

CITATIONS

Another section exclusive to books participating in the Search Inside program is the "Citations" section, although this only appears on certain Book Detail Pages. For example, you will notice that the Book Detail Page for *Self-Publishing Simplified* has the "Citations" section while the Book Detail Page for *Sell Your Book on Amazon* does not.

When writing the first edition of *Sell Your Book on Amazon*, I tried an experiment intending to get my book placed highly on the citations list for *The Self-Publishing Manual*.

Allow me to explain further: *The Self-Publishing Manual*, by Dan Poynter, was cited by 113 different books at the time I was writing the first edition. One book cited it nine times. My goal, therefore, was to appear on the top of that list by citing *The Self-Publishing Manual*, in context, ten times within the pages of *Sell Your Book on Amazon*.

Was that experiment successful? Visit *The Self-Publishing Manual* page and see if it worked. You will notice that, even though I cited *The Self-Publishing Manual* a total of ten times, one more than the next book, *Sell Your Book on Amazon* was not (and still is not) listed on the Book Detail Page in the "Citations" section. Why? Most likely this is due to the fact that Amazon adds and removes new functionality all the time and now, it appears Amazon's Search Inside algorithm is no longer tracking or calculating data related to citations. Bummer!

BOOKS ON RELATED TOPICS

Next is a relatively new section called "Books on Related Topics," which more clearly defines your competitive network. It is somewhat related to other sections that showcase competitive books, although unlike the others, this section showcases opportunities that may not yet be explored, because these suggestions are based upon content, rather than purchases by Amazon customers.

Identify your promotional opportunities based upon the books that appear in this section, and realize that your goal is to get your book listed in the "Books on Related Topics" section on your competitive books' Detail Pages.

WHAT DO CUSTOMERS...

Below "Books on Related Topics" is a section that displays the percentage of people who buy your book, or a competing book, after viewing your Book Detail Page. You always want to get the percentage of people buying your book as high as possible.

This data tells you in a statistical, quantifiable way whether or not your Book Detail

As you make changes to your Book Detail Page, the percentage of people buying your book may rise or fall. If the percentage increases, you know the change was a positive one.

Page is converting browsers to buyers. As you make changes to your Book Detail Page, this percentage may rise or fall. If the percentage increases, you know the change was a positive one. If the percentage decreases, you know the change was a poor one and you should revert to what you had before.

You can use this information to find competitive books for your competitive network. You can also study the tactics being employed by those books and ask yourself questions designed to help you improve your own effectiveness.

For instance, how did the people viewing your Book Detail Page discover those competitive books? The fact that someone looked at your Book Detail Page and yet bought a different book tells you that the authors (or publishers or promoters) of those books are doing something right. They have put steps into action and as a result, people who came to *your* book page ended up buying *their* book. Good for them; bad for you.

You want the exact opposite to take place. You want people to arrive upon *their* Book Detail Page due to *their* promotional efforts. Then you want them to discover your book, due to your Amazon marketing efforts. You want them to visit *your* Book Detail Page and purchase *your* book instead.

Obviously, it goes without saying that reviews play a large role here and that writing a good book plays an important role in receiving positive reviews. These Amazon marketing tactics can help a good book sell well for a long time, but can only help a poor book sell somewhat better for a short time.

Below the list displaying what customers ultimately buy is a link that says, **Explore similar items.** There even used to be a button that said **Compare these items,** which led to a page featuring side-by-side comparisons of the books people bought instead of (or in addition to) yours. By comparing similar titles you could draw correlations between the professional and aesthetic nature of the covers, the number of reviews they received, and so forth. All that information was helpful, but alas, Amazon no longer appears to offer it.

This comparison chart also provided a qualitative and quantitative basis by which to moderate your tactics—qualitative in that the chart provided demonstrable examples of quality (the cover art and the five-star reviews), and quantitative because you could witness the relationship between your sales rank and your competitors'. Obviously, you want to have the highest sales rank among all of your competitors. If you don't (and you rarely will), you have work to do.

It goes without saying that reviews play a large role here and that writing a good book plays an important role in receiving positive reviews.

Why would you want to advertise and promote competitive books on your Listmania Lists and Amazon Guides if those books are already more successful than yours? That question is self-defeating.

Now you might ask, "Why would I want to advertise and promote competitive books on my Listmania List or in my Amazon Guide if those books are already selling more copies than mine?" That question is self-defeating, and you want to remove that sort of thinking from your mind. Instead ask yourself, "How can I duplicate the successful things those books are doing?" An even better question is, "How can I leverage the success of those books for my own gain?"

All the people visiting your competitive books' Detail Pages have the same problem. They want to learn how to publish, cook, exercise, succeed, etc. While some may be predisposed to buying your competition's book simply because they have heard about it elsewhere, many more are not committed to any specific title—they just want the best book available that solves their problem. Your book needs to be *better* in the qualitative sense. If your book is better and people discover your book when looking at a competitor's, they will invariably purchase yours. The way they learn about yours is through competitive networking.

Remember, you aren't the only author pursuing these tactics. Many authors recognize the value of competitive networking on Amazon. If your book appears in the same circles as Competitor A, then the author of Competitor B will also mention you in her List-mania Lists and Amazon Guides. Now digital leverage starts taking off. Encourage more of it by adding Competitor B to your Amazon Friends network (see Chapter Two).

TAG THIS PRODUCT

Next on the Book Detail Page is a section devoted to product tags. For most people, tagging a product is a convenience factor more than anything. Once you tag a product with a particular term, you easily have the ability to find similarly tagged products later. As you tag multiple products with the same term, Amazon starts to create an index of products.

How does tagging a product help you as a book marketer? According to current theories in search engine optimization, tagging a product is an effective way to add a particular search keyword to your product. And the more people who tag your book with the same keyword, the more applicable that keyword becomes in reference to your book.

You want your book to have multiple tag words but all of them should be applicable to your book. The advantage to tagging multiple times is that each tag is listed on the Book Detail Page. In essence, you are suggesting other tag terms to other people, because the best-case scenario is if multiple people tag your book with the same keyword. The more tags your book receives for a particular keyword, the more Amazon's engine believes that keyword to be appropriate for your book and therefore, the higher your book will place in the search results for that term.

★★★★★   **SELL A DIGITAL VERSION...**

Below the tagging section, Amazon has a small section devoted to upselling (or at least promoting) their Kindle e-book reader and their complementary e-book store.

While the wording of this section often changes, the benefits have improved with Amazon's commitment to promoting the Kindle. Amazon Kindle editions enable you to sell a different edition of your book for a different price (typically cheaper), which in turn may turn into a hard copy sale.

You definitely want to upload a Kindle edition of your book if it is black-and-white and not very heavy on the graphics. Currently the Kindle is only capable of showing images in black-and-white, and the more complex your formatting, the more difficult time Amazon has converting your file to the Kindle in an aesthetic manner.

In fact, Kindle performs best with strictly black-and-white text and a minimum of formatting. What books fall into that category? Fiction. The Kindle is a fiction-writer's dream device because it helps level the playing field (at least a little) with nonfiction books, which historically have been much easier to promote and sell.

To upload a Kindle edition, go to Amazon's Digital Text Platform at dtp.amazon.com and

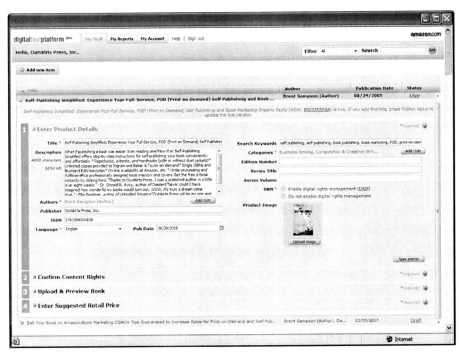

Fig. 8 - dtp.amazon.com

Keywords in the title help potential customers find your book and by using keywords not found in your hard copy editions, your Kindle Edition can help your work find a new audience.

create an account. You will need to provide banking information so Amazon can pay you. As I write this, Amazon is in the middle of adding support for international countries and is in the middle of modifying the payment structure for Kindle sales. As a result, I won't delve too deeply into the details concerning those factors.

Your first step is entering the "Product Details" for your Kindle edition, beginning with the title. You may use the same exact title you use for your hard copy format, or you may want to take advantage of the flexibility Amazon affords here by inserting some new keywords that you were unable to fit into your paperback or hardback title.

As discussed previously, keywords in the title help potential customers find your book. By using new keywords not found in your hard copy editions, your Kindle edition can help your work find a new audience.

The Digital Text Platform offers another opportunity to define the keywords for your Kindle edition in the "Search Keywords" field. Be sure to enter as many applicable keywords here as you can think of.

After completing all the required fields on the "Product Details" tab, all of which are relatively self-explanatory, proceed to the next step: "Confirm Content Rights."

Here you are indicating the territories for which you have the right to market and sell your book. You may either choose "Worldwide rights" or you can select from individual territories. Only you (or your publisher) know the answer to this question.

Next you confirm that you have all the rights required to make your content available for sale on the Kindle. Again, this is a question only you or your publisher can answer. It depends upon who published your book. Most (but not all) POD printers and publishers leave these rights in the author's hands, but check your publishing agreement to be sure.

The third step is uploading your book and then previewing it. The success you have with converting an electronic file to an aesthetically pleasing Kindle edition will depend on a number of factors, including the source of the original electronic file, and the complexity of the formatting.

The last step is setting a retail price. The minimum price is $0.99. When setting your price, consider the price of your hard copy formats and ask yourself whether you want your Kindle edition to cannibalize those sales (in which case you would set the retail price lower), or whether you want your Kindle edition to augment those sales by offering an-

The success you have converting an electronic file to an aesthetically pleasing Kindle edition will depend upon a number of factors, including the complexity of the formatting.

other platform choice for your customer (in which case you would set the retail price to be comparable with the hard copy).

Suffice it to say, this is certainly a tactic I recommend, particularly with the Kindle "app" available on iTunes App store. Now, Kindle books are available on the iPhone, iPod Touch, and iPad, too.

★★★★★   RATE THIS ITEM

Below the "Digital Version" section, Amazon asks you to rate your book to improve the personal recommendations Amazon shares with you. This is one of the methods Amazon employs to dynamically personalize your experience.

For example, if you give my *Self-Publishing Simplified* page a five-star rating, Amazon will remember that you like books on publishing and will start to mention other products in that same category. If you subsequently rank *The Self-Publishing Manual* and *Writer's Market* highly as well, Amazon really begins to build your profile. As a result, you receive more applicable recommendations both through the Amazon website and through email (if you have activated that function).

There are two things to keep in mind in regard to rating products.

- You want everyone who sees your page to rate it highly; so make sure your page is helpful.
- You should rank your own page highly so that your personal Amazon experience duplicates that of your target market.

CUSTOMER REVIEWS

Customer reviews are a valuable and powerful element of Amazon. Books without reviews do not receive the gold-star indicator near the title. Furthermore, books lacking that indicator look void in comparison to those that feature it. Therefore, the first thing you want to do when your book is listed on Amazon is get it reviewed. It is not sending much of a positive message to people looking at your book if they do not see any reviews on Amazon. Simply put, the more positive reviews there are for your book, the more apt people are to buy it.

In marketing, this concept is called *jumping on the bandwagon*. People like what other people like. You are more apt to go to a restaurant that has a full parking lot than one that has an empty parking lot, even if it means standing in line and getting inferior service. People, by nature, gravitate toward popular restaurants, music, movies, and books.

Encourage as many people as possible to write positive reviews for your book on Amazon. You should find ways to give readers an incentive to do it. The whole point of giving away review copies is to get a review. So if you give books away for reviews, ask those reviewers to post their reviews on Amazon. If you give away copies for marketing or promotional purposes, include a request for those readers to write a positive review on Amazon as well.

Yes, diplomatically suggest that they write a positive review because that is what you want. There is no harm in saying, "I would really appreciate a five-star review on Amazon." If you put it into their mind that you would prefer a positive review, you increase the likelihood of getting a high score. By the same token, if they read your book and feel inclined to give it a poor review, perhaps they will think twice before posting a review at all. In all likelihood, you will already have enough people who do not think you have a five-star book. Why pour fuel on the fire?

The whole point of giving away review copies is to get a review. So if you give books away for reviews, ask those reviewers also to post their reviews on Amazon.

Five-star reviews help your book sales and one-star reviews damage your book sales. A one-star review is worse than no review at all. Not only does Amazon use customer reviews to prioritize your book's popularity, but the quantity and quality of the reviews play a powerful role in converting a browser into a buyer. The more reviews your book has, the more popular your book becomes. Similarly, the more five-star reviews your book has, the more valuable Amazon thinks your book is.

> Five-star reviews help your book and one-star reviews damage your book. A one-star review is worse than no review at all.

Amazon is an indispensable tool for the online book marketer because Amazon recommends products. If somebody comes onto Amazon to buy Product A, Amazon will not consider the transaction a success unless that person also purchases Product B. Presumably, the customer learned about Product B through Amazon's recommendations.

For example, people will come to Amazon looking for a book about publishing. They will look at various Book Detail Pages featuring books about publishing. On each of those pages, they may see a reference to *Self-Publishing Simplified*, or they may see a reference to me. Amazon is recommending my book to them in a variety of different ways. This is similar to a bookstore employee handing my book to a customer and saying, "Here, you might also like this."

Amazon does the hard part for you by exposing your book to readers who are pre-qualified to buy it.

Or, perhaps they do not see a reference to *Self-Publishing Simplified*. Perhaps, instead, they see a reference to *The Complete Guide to Self-Publishing*, or *The Self-Publishing Manual*. Those books receive the recommendation, but I may still receive exposure since a link to me or my book ideally appears on the Book Detail Pages of all books within my competitive network, including those two.

Here is the bottom line: Amazon exposes your book to readers who are already pre-qualified to buy it. A bookstore employee would not hand my book to a reader scanning the pages of *Harry Potter and the Deathly Hallows*. Amazon does the hard part for you, which is finding pre-qualified buyers, people who have demonstrated an interest in your subject matter based upon their previous shopping habits. Amazon presents your book as another option they might consider.

Customer reviews play a large part in how Amazon selects the books it recommends to other people. Since Amazon's primary goal is to close the sale, Amazon is more inclined to recommend books that many people reviewed and many people liked.

When you look at the customer review section, you will see the same elements for each reviewer, including the review score, the headline, the date, and the actual review.

Underneath each review are **Yes** and **No** buttons that invite readers to vote on the helpfulness of the review. Since Amazon likes seeing a lot of reviews that other people find helpful, you want to vote *Yes* for every five-star review your book receives.

A book that receives many five-star reviews that are rated as helpful by many other people is a book Amazon will recognize as one that is valuable to its shoppers. Amazon is programmed to recommend books that have positive activity. Having numerous positive and helpful reviews increases the chance of your book receiving exposure somewhere else on Amazon's site.

Since reviews appear in reverse chronological order, you want to make sure your most recent review is a five-star review. Ultimately, you do not have any control over what other people write. But since most people will only look at the first few reviews on the front page, your goal is to ensure that those reviews are positive. Rarely will someone read more than the first five or six reviews.

If you have a particularly unfair and negative review, you can attempt to have it removed administratively by sending an email to **community-help@amazon.com.**

> Having numerous positive and helpful reviews increases the chance of your book receiving exposure somewhere else on Amazon.

★★★   CUSTOMER DISCUSSIONS

Below the "Customer Reviews" section is the "Customer Discussions" section. These are divided into two categories: a forum for your book, and forums on topics Amazon believes are related to your book.

Anyone can start a discussion, either specific to your book, or on a related topic, and anyone else can join that discussion. The more discussion topics on your book, the more Amazon recognizes activity surrounding your book.

Along the right side of the discussion categories are community groups related to your book. Amazon identifies applicable groups based upon the tags associated with your book. The more tags you have for a specific keyword, the more likely it is that your book will be exposed to community participants.

Participating in discussions and communities takes a lot of time. You want to make sure it is time that pays off.

Create a topic for your book and post it. Then check back once in a while to see if anybody responded to your post. Soon you may find yourself with a really active forum. Be as helpful and informed as possible when posting comments or replies to other people. Imagine how helpful your nonfiction book must be if your discussion posting is help-ful *and* free! Or imagine how fun your fiction book must be if your postings are always fas-cinating and filled with prose that sparkles. These are the reactions you want people to have when reading the postings in the "Cus-tomer Discussions" section.

LISTMANIA!

The next section is "Listmania," where you will see three different Listmania Lists, each covering a topic similar to that of the book you are viewing. So, in the case of *Self-Publishing Simplified,* the Listmania Lists cen-ter on publishing and writing. The lists that appear are determined by Amazon based upon its belief that the lists will appeal to visitors on the page.

If your Book Detail Page does not have a "Listmania" section, it means Amazon does not know enough about your book to create an applicable list. Whether or not a Listma-nia List appears on your Book Detail Page is irrelevant, because other people's Listmania Lists on your page won't help you sell more books. But you want to be sure that the List-mania Lists you create appear on other books' Detail Pages, and it helps if those books are popular. Chapter Four discusses that tactic in more detail along with some recent changes to the guidelines.

★★★★★   ## SO YOU'D LIKE TO...

Below Listmania is the "So You'd Like To..." section. I discuss So You'd Like To... Guides in depth in Chapter Five.

As far as the Book Detail Page goes, this section is similar to Listmania. Three guides are shown, all of them on a topic similar to the subject matter of the book being viewed. The guides that appear here are determined by Amazon's algorithm of what is most likely to appeal to visitors of the page.

★★★   ## AMAPEDIA COMMUNITY

This section used to be called "Product Wiki" before it was renamed.

Amapedia is Amazon's version of Wikipedia and was in beta at the time of my first edition in 2007 and is *still* in beta as of 2010. I wouldn't be surprised if it disappeared altogether soon. You can explore it at **www.amapedia.com**

One of the defining characteristics of a wiki is that it is factual, not subjective. Subjective opinions have no place in a wiki and are better left in the customer review or discussion sections. Most wiki posts are moderated to some extent to ensure that factual,

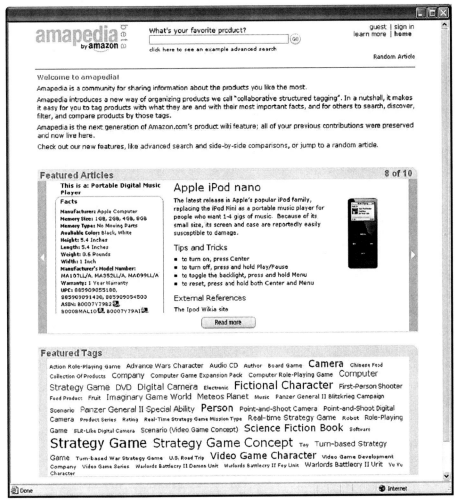

Fig. 9 - www.amapedia.com

useful information is supplied. Users supply information in their field of expertise about a particular topic. It is self-policing and self-regulating, which means if you were to post inaccurate information, other people would (presumably) correct you by editing your content with their own.

If you do not yet have an Amapedia posting for your book, you should create one. Be factual.

Amapedia hasn't changed much in three years and it is anyone's guess as to whether it will soon receive attention from Amazon, or disappear entirely. But it takes so little time to create a listing on Amapedia, it's a relatively easy tactic to complete.

★★★★   LOOK FOR SIMILAR ITEMS

The last sections of the Book Detail Page involve category and subject lists of similar items based upon the category or subject matter of the book. You want your book to be in as many categories as possible. Amazon categorizes your book based upon its BISAC codes. BISAC stands for Book Industry Standards and Communications. This defines the conventions whereby book data is shared. Most publishers submit at least three

BISAC codes and Amazon sometimes adds additional BISAC codes based upon what it knows about your book.

Looking for similar items is an efficient way to add titles to your competitive network. Get information about the top ten books that appear on these lists. Make a concerted effort to expose your book on their Book Detail Pages. Focus on these books in Listmania Lists and use these books in your Amazon Guides.

Most people spend more time
and energy going around problems
than in trying to solve them.

- Henry Ford

CHAPTER 4

LISTMANIA!

What is Listmania? Listmania is a five-star marketing tactic on Amazon, similar to a top ten list. Listmania lets you pick forty products from Amazon and create a list of those products based upon a common theme that you define. When it comes to promoting your book, the idea behind a Listmania List is to pick products that will appeal to your demographics and simultaneously attract as many people as possible.

If you do not know who your audience is, you must solve that mystery first. Who is reading your book? Who is the audience?

Once you have your reader well in mind, create a list of forty products designed to appeal to that person. Yes, you may even choose to include your book on your list, although you should be warned that if you do, Amazon may choose to remove your list administratively in light of recent (and harsh) guidelines.

Now let's walk through the process by clicking on the **Create a Listmania! List** link within the "Listmania" section of the Book Detail Page.

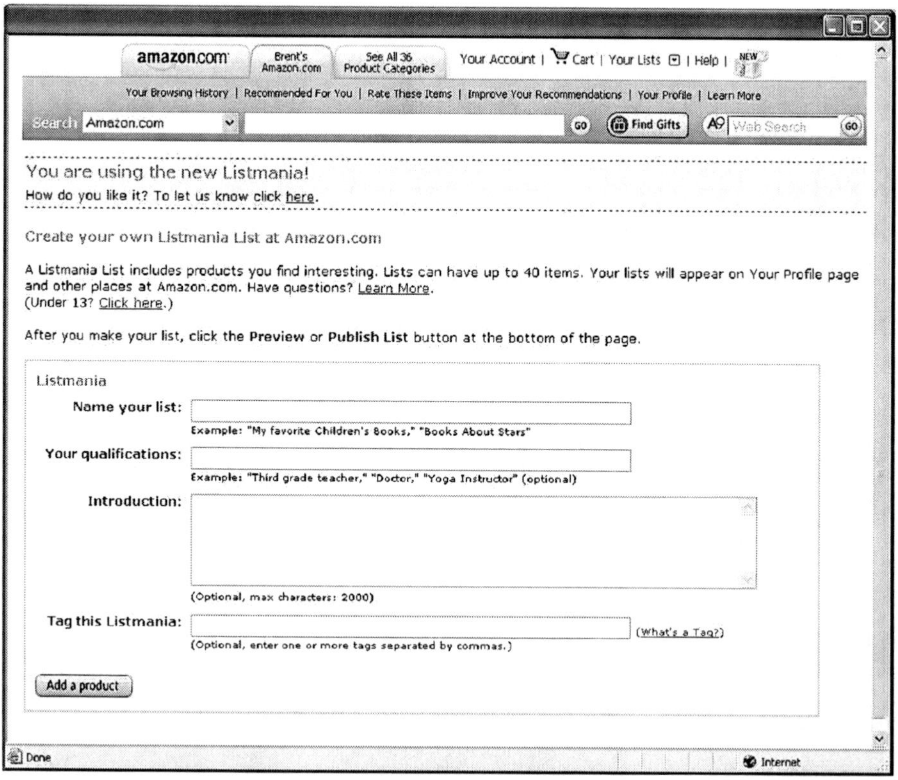

Fig. 10 - www.amazon.com/listmania

NAME YOUR LIST

You want a catchy name that is also as descriptive and accurate as possible. People like lists with numbers in them, so title your list thusly:

- Top 10 meals you can cook in 10 minutes
- 25 perfect gifts for a little girl
- 7 habits of successfully published people

YOUR QUALIFICATIONS

What qualifies you to create this list? If you are creating a list about cooking and you are a chef, then state that here. If your lone qualification is that you are the author of your published book, that's fine. Having a published book on a subject certainly entitles you to create a Listmania List on that subject.

For example, if you published a horror novel, then your qualifications for your horror list should include more than the title; you should also mention the genre as a part of your qualifications. For example: "Author of the thrilling horror novel *The Horror.*"

If you have a conversion rate of 2%, you will sell two books if 100 people see your Book Detail Page. You will sell 20,000 books if one million people see it.

Your overall goal is to increase the amount of exposure your name and your book's title receive on other Amazon Book Detail Pages. The more exposure you receive, the more eyeballs see it. Everything is about maximizing your impressions, the number of unique people who see your Book Detail Page on Amazon.

Selling is a numbers game, based upon statistics. If statistics tell you that 2% of the people who learn about your book buy it, you have a conversion rate of 2%. So if one hundred people learn about your book, you are going to sell two books. If one million people learn about your book, you are going to sell twenty thousand books. Ultimately, then, your goal is twofold. You want to increase the conversion rate and increase the number of unique people learning about your book. Chapter Three discusses tactics to increase your conversion rate. Listmania Lists, on the other hand, are very good at increasing the number of people who learn about your book.

INTRODUCTION

Why are you creating this list? A bad answer is, "To sell copies of my book." You want to define a problem your demographic group experiences and then indicate within your introduction how your list provides the solution to their problem.

Perhaps ask a question first: "Are you finding it impossible to make as much money as you would like selling your book on Amazon?" Then offer a solution: "Below are the top 40 books on the subject of self-publishing the right way so you can control your Amazon profit margin!"

The beautiful part about Amazon is that it will only present your list to people who answer "yes" to your question. It pre-qualifies people for you, because it shows your list only to people who would be interested in the products on your list to begin with. As long as your question is directly related to the products you show, the answer to your question will always be *yes*.

ADD A PRODUCT

When you click the **Add a product** button, a pop-up box asks you to search for the product you want to add. Yes, you can add products other than books to your Listmania List, and you should in due time. We'll discuss that a bit later. But first, let's add a book together.

Conduct a search under "All Products" for *Self-Publishing Simplified*. My book appears at the top of a short list. To the left of my book is a small **Select** button. Click **Select** and my book is added to your Listmania List.

Want to add *The Self-Publishing Manual*, *Writer's Market*, or *The Complete Guide to Self-Publishing*? Repeat the process for each book you wish to add.

What could be easier? Naturally you should add books within *your* competitive network, not mine. The books I mentioned above are a good selection if your book is about book publishing or marketing, but a bad selection if you are selling a cookbook, a diet book, or a horror novel.

ADDING COMMENTS

Once you add a product to your list, Amazon asks you to complete a comments section. You do not have to enter anything here, but you should. The comments for all the products on your lists should be general and positive in nature. If you include your book in your list, the comment for your book should be in the form of a *hook*. A hook is a very succinct collection of five or six words that attract attention.

Typically, your hook should be in the form of a question containing the word "you." "You" is the most powerful word in marketing. Combining the word *you* with a question is an effective way of engaging people. "Do you ever...?" "Have you...?" "What if you could...?" These are forms of questions that have the word *you* in them—and they are all hooks. You want to find a problem that your book is going to solve. Put that problem in the form of a question in your book's comments section.

If this is the same hook that you feature on the back cover of your book, that's great! Now you are branding your message across different platforms.

ORDERING YOUR LIST

As you start to add more products, you should arrange them in a strategic order. The arrows allow you to move products up and down on your list.

Why is the order of your Listmania List important? Because the product in the top spot generally receives the most exposure. If your list contains a book by somebody more famous than you, and it should, then consider featuring *that* book in the number one spot, simply because doing so may increase the number of people who elect to view your list. Obviously, the order will be determined on a list-by-list basis.

Yes, you will be making many Listmania Lists. But your *first* Listmania List can be easy, such as a top ten list. Ultimately, every list you make should feature the maximum number of products, which is forty. When you start creating lists with products other than books, you really expand your demographics, and therefore your exposure, on Amazon.

Always consider the typical reader for your book when creating your list. Then, consider other books or products that your target readers might enjoy. If they are interested in my book *Self-Publishing Simplified,* they might also be interested in *The Self-Publishing Manual* by Dan Poynter, for example.

When I began creating lists to market *Sell Your Book on Amazon,* I included *1001 Ways to Market Your Books* by John Kremer. Do you see? The books you add to your list always target the same demographic as your book.

Once you have forty books or products on your Listmania List, determine which book/product should be in the top spot. If

When you start creating lists with products other than books, you really expand your demographics, and therefore your exposure, on Amazon.

you are choosing to include your own book, refrain from including it in the top spot. You may not be as famous as the authors of the other books you add. Or your book may not be as popular. Ultimately, the goal is to get people to read your Listmania List. The way to get them to do that is by presenting them with something they recognize (e.g., a famous book by a famous author). Once they are reading your list, you can push them toward your book more aggressively through the comments section. But the first step is getting them to your list in the first place. Swallow your pride and select the best book to get the job done.

Potential customers are going to read your Listmania List because they are interested in the name of your list, or because they are interested in the book cover representing your list. If you have forty books on your list, none of which is well-known, your book may very well be the best choice to top the list. But it is possible that the books on your list may not be popular enough. The more popular the books or products are (defined by their sales rank) the more exposure your list will receive.

However, before basing your choice solely on a book's popularity, also consider each book's cover. Pick a cover that is the

> The goal is to get people to read your Listmania List. The way to get them to do that is by presenting them with a book they recognize. You may not be as famous or as popular as the authors of the books you add.

most appealing. Be unbiased and impartial. Ask other people to look at the books on your list and pick the cover that appeals to them the most.

HOW DO LISTMANIA LISTS HELP?

Let us look at an example of where Listmania Lists show up. This will help you understand the context in which they affect Amazon shoppers.

Visit my Book Detail Page for *Self-Publishing Simplified,* and scroll down past the reviews. Near the bottom, you will see a section called "Listmania" and within that section, you will see three Listmania Lists. These lists appear on my Book Detail Page because they match the subject matter of my book.

Amazon has determined that the people who come to my page will be interested in seeing these three Listmania Lists. When you create a Listmania List, Amazon displays your list on the Book Detail Pages viewed by your target audience. In order to make that determination, Amazon examines the subject matter for all the products on your list.

Once Amazon determines the applicable categories, it places your Listmania List on other applicable Book Detail Pages. When people viewing those other Book Detail Pages see your list, they may click on it to learn more.

Granted, they are also going to learn about the other products on your list, but that's okay. Do not make the mistake of *only* featuring your book in your Listmania List. That would be pointless. In fact, it is usually pointless to make a Listmania List with fewer than forty products since one of the ways Amazon determines where it should display your list is based upon the products that are a part of your list. The more products on your list, the more often your list appears. It is as simple as that.

Since Amazon has a tendency to display your list on the Book Detail Pages of the other books on your list, make sure some of the books you choose are popular. As you become more strategic about the way you create Listmania Lists, you should examine the popularity of each book based upon its sales rank and then upon its relevance to your book. The ideal books to add are those that rank high in both popularity and relevancy.

Create multiple lists to maximize results. Fortunately, Amazon makes it easy to modify your search results based upon a book's rank or relevance. Create a Listmania List com-

The ideal books to add to your Listmania Lists are those that rank high in popularity and relevancy. Examine the popularity of each book based upon its sales rank and then upon its relevance.

prised of books that are well-known. Then create a list based upon the relevance of other books in your category.

For example, if you wanted to create a List-mania List for your cookbook, you might create a list based upon the topic of Cajun cuisine. After conducting a search for "Cajun cooking," you would get the top forty books based upon their relevancy to "Cajun cooking." There's a Listmania List right there! All you need to do is follow the steps outlined above to duplicate those results onto your list.

To continue the example, your cookbook may cover more than just Cajun cooking. It may also cover Southwestern cooking and California cuisine. If so, do a Listmania List for each one of those subcategories, creating multiple lists with completely different products. Your book is the constant on every list you create.

Have you published multiple books? Consider including your related books within each of your Listmania Lists. Remember the concept of digital leverage I introduced earlier? Here is how it works: Your single Listmania List now promotes two or more of your books.

That said, keep in mind the recent changes to Listmania guidelines that authorize Amazon to remove Listmania Lists administratively if they appear to be too self-promo-

Keep in mind recent Listmania guidelines that authorize Amazon to remove Listmania Lists that appear to be too self-promotional.

tional. For example, when I was writing the first edition of this book, I created many lists that mentioned my own books. Eventually, those lists wound up being deleted by Amazon. Now I just focus on lists that appeal to my audience, knowing my signature link will drive customers to my profile and my books.

LISTMANIA POPULARITY

Amazon determines a list's popularity based upon the number of times it has been viewed and the number of times other shoppers have indicated it was helpful. Everything is a popularity contest on Amazon because Amazon strives to display information to people that other people have indicated an interest in. If your Listmania List is seen a lot, that is good. If it is considered helpful a lot, that is great.

Listmania offers the opportunity to vote on the helpfulness of each list. When you read a Listmania List, it shows you the list's statistics. It tells you the number of times people have viewed the list and it asks if you found the list helpful. Amazon isn't necessarily in the business to help you personally, but it is in the business to offer widespread assistance of a general nature.

So if people indicate that your Listmania List is helpful, your Listmania List will receive more exposure. Then more people will see it. The more people who see it, the more people will vote on its popularity. The more popular it is, the more exposure it gets, and so on, and so forth in a virtuous circle.

CHAPTER 5

SO YOU'D LIKE TO... GUIDES

So You'd Like To... Guides have a rather clunky name, so I am going to shorten such references to Amazon Guides for the sake of this book. Just know that when I refer to the Amazon Guides, I am referring to what Amazon calls the So You'd Like To... Guides.

Presumably, the name for this function is in the context of "So, you'd like to be a movie star" or "So, you'd like to marry a millionaire"; and in that light, the name fits its purpose. If you want to be a movie star or marry a millionaire, you might find a guide that offers such instructions inviting. In fact, Amazon has made it easy to create a hook for your guide by naming it thusly. Amazon Guides are a five-star tactic.

As I mentioned earlier, an effective hook uses the word *you* and identifies a problem, which thereby implies you have a solution. "So, you'd like to be a movie star" implies a problem (you must not be a movie star yet...) and it implies a solution (by reading this information, you will learn how to become a movie star).

By the same token, "So, you'd like to marry a millionaire" implies a problem (you must be unwed or married to a person of less desirable means...) and it implies the solution (by reading this information, you will learn the steps involved in marrying a millionaire).

WHAT IS AN AMAZON GUIDE?

An Amazon Guide is an article that references products on Amazon under the pretext of providing information or entertainment. In order for your guide to be effective, the content must be relevant to your book, since the purpose of the guide is to sell your book. Amazon's purpose is to display guides that both educate and identify lots of other products. It is Amazon's hope that people will learn about new products by reading your guide. What a coincidence! That is your hope, too, as long as one of those new products is yours. When you find common goals with Amazon, you will find success.

Here is how the Amazon Guides work in a nutshell: Write an article related to your book and create an Amazon Guide using that article. By referring to books within the body of the guide, associate your article with your book and other related books.

You want to associate your expertise with as many similar (i.e., competitive) books as possible. Keep in mind that the products you identify are not limited solely to books. As you become more comfortable creating guides, you should mention other products, as well—anything that interests the audience for your book. But for the purposes of your first Amazon Guide, stick with books.

Browse the books within your competitive network to determine the best ones to include in your first guide. Chapter Three details several methods for locating books within your competitive network.

Or you may perform an Amazon search for books to include in your guide. Or you may choose to duplicate the titles you used within one of your Listmania Lists. In fact,

Write an article related to your book and create an Amazon Guide using that article. By referring to books within the body of the guide, associate your article with your book and other related books.

Make note of the ISBNs you use in your first Listmania List. Once you complete your list, use those same products in your first Amazon Guide.

you can complete a list and a guide simultaneously by making note of the ISBNs for the products within one of your Listmania Lists. Once you complete your list, use those same products in your Amazon Guide. Doing this doubles the chances of your guide or list appearing on other Book Detail Pages.

Obviously, you want to create original guides, too, without repeating the same products. This increases the total number of products associated with your promotional tactics. Ultimately, you want to have as many products identified in all of your guides as possible.

Therefore, you need to create multiple guides. You must also write multiple articles since each guide should feature a different article to some degree. Creating guides means creating content. Fortunately, there are tricks to doing this. You have written a book, haven't you? A "guide" is just another word for an excerpt from your book.

As a fiction writer, your guides can be short stories. Find a chapter in your novel that has a beginning, middle, and end. Use that chapter as a guide. Who knows? Maybe you can become the expert on creating short stories in your Amazon Guides. If you do anything often enough, people start to associate you with that activity. That is one of the fundamental steps toward branding yourself and establishing yourself as an expert.

Nonfiction guides are more cut and dry. The chapters of your book are probably divided into parts already. If you have written a cookbook, you may have a series of categories into which your recipes fall. There could be an Amazon Guide for each recipe type. If you have a chapter on Cajun cooking, for example, create a guide on Cajun recipes.

The purpose of your guide is to share something valuable, so include the full recipe. Then refer to your cookbook and other cookbooks within your guide for additional recipes. Broaden the scope of your guide beyond cooking. For example, "If you like this recipe, you may also be interested in this book about shrimp, or this book about New Orleans, or even this Crock-Pot," etc. The idea here is to find connections between your guide and other products, thereby widening your publicity net and establishing your expertise in a particular field or genre.

SIMILARITIES WITH LISTMANIA

Obviously, there are similarities between Listmania Lists and Amazon Guides. They both increase exposure of you and your book. Similarly, the products you mention are instrumental in determining which Book Detail Pages display your list or guide. You should also be careful with your choice of books. As with Listmania, recent guideline changes allow Amazon administratively to remove guides that are determined to be overtly self-promotional.

DIFFERENCES WITH LISTMANIA

The main difference between a Listmania List and an Amazon Guide is the difficulty in creating one. A Listmania List is fairly easy from a creative standpoint. You do not have to write anything. Instead, you simply decide upon forty products and create a Listmania List. Amazon does the majority of the work for you.

On the other hand, Amazon Guides require some content, and the content needs to be relevant to the subject of your book or to your expertise as an author. The good news is that, as an author, you have already written this content. That's right—your book!

The difficulty in creating an Amazon Guide is also one of its greatest advantages. Since they are more difficult to make, there are fewer guides on Amazon competing with your guide. Human nature dictates that easy tasks will always be done more frequently than hard tasks.

If you make the effort to create a popular, well-written Amazon Guide, you will face less competition and, therefore, gain more exposure. This is all about getting your guide exposed. To that end, let's walk through the process of creating an Amazon Guide step-by-step.

CREATING A TITLE

You create Amazon Guides from the "So You'd Like To..." section of your Book Detail Page. Click on the link that says, "Create a guide."

The first section concerns the title of your guide. All titles begin with the words "So You'd Like To..." Amazon is branding this product.

Let's look at an actual guide that I created to promote *Self-Publishing Simplified*.

The guide is titled, "So You'd Like To Publish Your Book." If someone interested in publishing a book sees my guide while looking at other publishing books, he might be inclined to click on it. Up comes an article that I have written to help choose a profitable publishing path. In the body of the guide, I mention two of my books. I also mention other books, including *The Self-Publishing Manual* and *Writer's Market*.

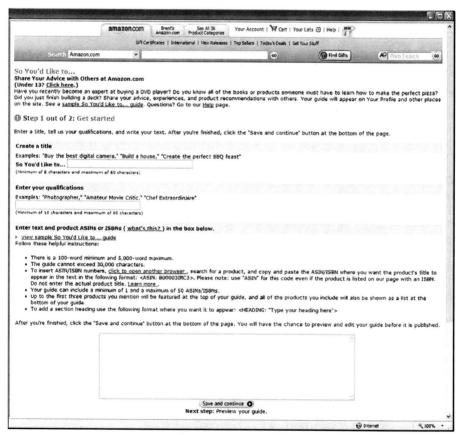

Fig. 11 - www.amazon.com/sylt

Since these books are highly relevant and highly ranked, their familiarity reinforces the applicability of the guide and grants it legitimacy. Now I am more of an expert in the minds of the people reading my guide. People like buying nonfiction books from experts. All of these elements are uniting together to sell more copies of my book, even if I don't add my own book to the guide.

ENTERING YOUR QUALIFICATIONS

The next section of the guide creation page reads, "Enter your qualifications." You should use your personal hook here. You have only a short amount of space in which to summarize your qualifications, so make each word count.

Whatever hook you use should be a part of every promotion tool Amazon offers. Maintain consistency by repeating the same phrase over and over. Give some thought to what your signature, or in other words your *headline,* will be before you start any of these exercises. Write it down, and make sure it fits in all of these forms so it can always stay exactly the same.

ENTERING YOUR TEXT & PRODUCTS

The last section of the guide creation page involves supplying your article and product identification numbers. There is a 100-word minimum and a 5,000-word maximum for the length of your guide. Adding products to your guide is similar to adding products to your Listmania List. You use a search box to locate products based upon a keyword search, and then add selected products into the body of your guide.

As usual, it helps if these products are either applicable to your book in some way, or appeal strongly to your demographic. Do a topic search, and then do a similar search based upon relevancy and then based upon sales rank. Ultimately, you want to feature products that are not only relevant to your book but are also valued by many people, since that increases the likelihood of the most appropriate people (potential customers) seeing your guide.

Once you create a guide and save it, Amazon places your guide on Book Detail Pages it thinks have the most relevance. Amazon bases this determination on the products you put inside your guide and also on the subject matter of those products. People interested in your book will see your guides.

You want to feature products that are not only relevant to your book but are also valued by many people, since that increases the liklihood of people seeing your guide.

Therefore, you want the products within your guide to be appealing. You also want the products to be popular and connected to your book or your expertise.

The more popular the products are, the more popular the Book Detail Pages are. That means their pages will be viewed more often, which means your Guide will be viewed more often. A guide that is viewed more often is read more often and voted as valuable more often. The sum total is more exposure, and exposure is what leads to people buying your book.

As with the Listmania guidelines, Amazon recently added rules to the creation of Amazon Guides that allow Amazon to remove guides that appear to be too self-promotional. So while you are able to add your own book to your guide, doing so increases your risk of having your guide removed entirely from Amazon. A more conservative approach would be to focus solely on other books or products that appeal to your demographic, and have your signature link, in other words your headline, (which appears at the top of your guide) do the selling for you.

You must do the thing you think you cannot do.

- Eleanor Roosevelt

CHAPTER 6

ADDITIONAL AMAZON POSSIBILITIES

The possibilities for promoting your book do not stop with Listmania and So You'd Like To...Guides. Amazon offers many more resources devoted to helping an author sell books. You will find these resources within a page titled the Publishers and Book Sellers Guide at **www.amazon.com/publishers**

PUBLISHERS & BOOK SELLERS GUIDE

The first link, **List Your Title,** provides instructions for listing your book through Amazon's Advantage program, through the Mar-

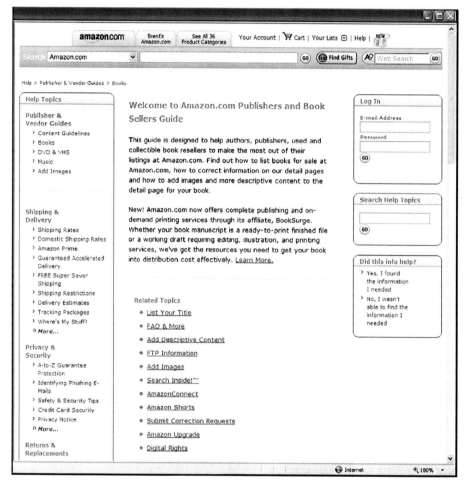

Fig. 12 - www.amazon.com/publishers

ketplace section, or through Amazon's on-demand publisher, CreateSpace. It may still say "BookSurge" on the Amazon site, but late in 2009, Amazon retired the "Book-Surge" name and will be publishing exclusively under CreateSpace by the time you read this, even if lingering references to "BookSurge" remain.

I discussed Advantage and Marketplace thoroughly in Chapters One and Three, respectively. CreateSpace offers pros and cons, too. The positive, of course, is CreateSpace's close alliance with Amazon. Ironically, this is also CreateSpace's biggest disadvantage.

The only way to get a CreateSpace book distributed outside of Amazon, say onto Barnes & Noble's competitive website, or any other book retailer's website for that matter, is to absorb a staggering 60% trade discount on those outlets. That's 5% *worse* than the 55% you're forced to pay through Amazon Advantage and single-handedly dissolves all the advantages of short-discounting your book through POD online wholesalers.

Adding insult to injury, this profit-prohibitive EDC ("Enhanced Distribution Channel" as CreateSpace calls it) plan also applies to Ingram. Ingram is the largest book wholesaler in the United States.

Since nearly all print-on-demand publishers list their books on Amazon, and most of them also include distribution via Ingram at the same profit margin for the author, you may find that the CreateSpace disadvantages outweigh its advantages.

The **FAQ & More** link answers specific questions about listing procedures.

> The only way to get a CreateSpace book distributed outside of Amazon, say onto Barnes & Noble, is to absorb a staggering 60% trade discount.

FTP is an acronym for File Transfer Protocol. In this case, FTP involves the transfer of book content and images from your personal computer to Amazon's servers.

The **Add Descriptive Content** link provides you with an online method for enhancing the information on your Book Detail Page. Any information the publisher failed to provide when your book was originally listed with Amazon can be added here by you. As discussed in Chapter Three, you should add as much information as you can. Follow the **Book Content Update Form** link on the Add Descriptive Content page.

First you supply information about yourself, your mailing address, and the book's publisher. You also need to specify the book's ISBN. Once that preliminary form is complete, you proceed to a longer form to provide more information.

A word of advice and caution: This form does not allow you to override data originally supplied by the publisher. Amazon will always give preference to the data from the original or official source. Chapter Three includes additional hints about this form.

Under the "Add Descriptive Content" menu is a link for **FTP Information**.

FTP is an acronym for File Transfer Protocol, which involves the transfer of data from one computer to another. In this case, FTP involves the transfer of either book content or book images from your personal computer to Amazon's servers.

Amazon has recently altered their procedure for receiving images and information. Now, most uploads, including those for the Search Inside program, are conducted through the Seller Central interface. In fact, the FTP Information page accessible from the Publishers and Book Sellers Guide is blank.

Next comes **Add Images.** Chapter Three discusses the reasons for adding images on a strategic level. Seller Central helps you on a more tactical level. Visit **sellercentral.amazon.com** for details.

Inside the Book is the fifth link on the Publishers and Book Sellers Guide. This link displays further information about Amazon's Search Inside the Book program, which I covered in Chapter Three.

To briefly reiterate, the concept of Search Inside is to mimic the experience of being in a bookstore. No matter how comfortable one is with shopping online, nothing satisfies that kinesthetic urge to pick up a book and flip through its pages.

Search Inside attempts to digitize that experience by allowing the user to view the first few pages of the book. You can even "flip it over" and see what the back cover looks like. This ability is integral to a successful shopping experience and summarizes one of the main advantages of Search Inside.

Only by participating in Search Inside does Amazon's search engine receive thorough details about your book.

Only the rights holder can apply for the Search Inside the Book program. Who the rights holder is depends upon how your book was published.

Perhaps even more advantageous is that all books participating in Search Inside receive a greater degree of scrutiny by Amazon's search engine. The more information Amazon has about you and your book, the better off you are.

Let's say your book has a rather archaic title that has nothing to do with your book's content. For starters, maybe you should have a different title for your book; but more importantly, only by participating in Search Inside does Amazon's search engine receive thorough details about your book. The content of your book is digitized in such a way that the engine can search the words inside your book and show your book to prospective buyers based on more than just the title or author's name.

The **Search Inside** link from the Publishers and Book Sellers Guide takes you to the sign-up form for the Search Inside the Book program. One of the first steps toward signing up is stating that you are the rights holder to your book. Only the rights holder can apply for the Search Inside program.

Who the rights holder is depends upon how your book was published. If you independently self-published your book or published your book with an on-demand publisher, you probably kept your rights.

If a mainstream publisher published your book or even if you published through a small independent publisher, chances are good that you lost the rights to your book.

Read your contract to be sure.   Then read the participation agreement for Search Inside, too. Confirm that you have the rights to your book before you participate in the Search Inside program, because you are stating on the form that you are the rights holder.

Once you complete the online form, you will receive an email with further information and instructions, including their request for a digital copy of your book. You may send them a PDF file of your book through Seller Central. It typically takes about six weeks for your book to be processed. Upon completion, your Book Detail Page will feature the "Search Inside" logo above your cover image.

The sixth link is **AmazonConnect**, which is now Author Central, and is covered in Chapter Two.

Next comes **Amazon Shorts**. The idea here is to encourage authors to write short stories or articles and publish them on Amazon. Readers interested in getting a sense of that writer's style can read the Amazon Short and decide whether or not they like the author enough to buy a whole book.

Amazon requires exclusive rights to Amazon Shorts for a minimum of six months.

Amazon Shorts should be between 2,000 and 10,000 words. Amazon requires the exclusive rights to your short story or article for a minimum of six months. If you have already published your "short" on your website or elsewhere, Amazon would consider that an infringement of this particular agreement—although it is also unlikely that they would care enough to investigate or pursue the matter.

Amazon markets the Amazon Shorts concept to authors as a moneymaking device, but it is hardly income producing. Shorts sell for $0.49 each, and the author receives 40% of that (roughly $0.20).

In spite of this barrier, you may decide writing Amazon Shorts is a good marketing tactic for you. Writing articles is one of the best ways to market your book, and Amazon offers a plethora of different ways to do just that—Amazon Shorts, Amazon Guides, and your Amazon Blog to name just three.

Beginning the Amazon Shorts process is easy. Send an email to **amazon-shorts@amazon.com.** You will receive an automated email in response that contains further information and instructions. Or visit the Shorts store at: **www.amazon.com/shorts**

The next link on the Publishers and Book Sellers Guide is **Submit Correction Request**.

Amazon Upgrade sells the digital version of your book to consumers who have already purchased the hard copy version.

This link provides suggestions for correcting basic information about a book, such as its title, author, binding, page count, publication date, or format/edition. The link for correcting this information is also found at the bottom of every Book Detail Page and I covered it in a little more detail in Chapter Three.

The next link, **Amazon Upgrade**, offers another way to make some revenue. In essence, Amazon Upgrade sells the digital version of your book to consumers who have already purchased the hard copy version.

Perhaps they have not received the hard copy yet, but they need some of the information immediately. They can upgrade for a nominal fee (of which you receive a percentage) and gain immediate access to the entire contents of your digitized file.

How nominal is the upgrade charge? It is determined by a convoluted calculation against the retail price of the hard copy. If your book is a non-trade title, Amazon starts with 10% of the retail price and then doubles it. For instance, Amazon takes 10% of a $10 retail price ($1) and doubles it ($2) to determine the upgrade fee to the consumer. Amazon starts with 5% of the retail price for trade titles. In either case, you split the upgrade fee with Amazon fifty-fifty.

> To calculate the upgrade fee, Amazon starts with 10% of the retail price for non-trade titles and then doubles it. For trade titles, Amazon starts with 5%.

With the notable exception of understanding the needlessly confusing contract, there is no additional work on your part, provided you have already submitted your book to the Search Inside program. If so, Amazon uses that content to facilitate the upgrade functionality.

Through Amazon Upgrade, shoppers can view, search, bookmark, and highlight the digital e-book edition of your book. They may also copy text from the book and print a certain number of pages. Even if a user fails to upgrade, they receive immediate access to 20% of your digital file for seven days after they purchase the hard copy edition as a free trial to motivate them to upgrade.

To get started, send an email to **digital-books@amazon.com.**

I tend to believe the Publishers and Book Sellers Guide is no longer accurate or up-to-date on Amazon's site. For instance, the blank page that occurs when clicking on FTP Information, the link to AmazonConnect (also defunct), and the mention of BookSurge, which folded into CreateSpace in 2009, suggest the content is dated.

As such, take away what you will from the above summary of the Publishers and Book Sellers Guide.

WHAT IS BXGY?

Up until 2009, one of the most expensive marketing opportunities at Amazon had the rather unfortunate moniker of BXGY, which stood for "Buy X, Get Y." Basically, you paid Amazon to list your book in association with another book. The cost depended upon the sales rank of the other book you chose. The higher the rank, the higher the cost. Pairing your book with a book ranked 250 or better cost $1,000 per month, while pairing with a book ranked 251 or worse cost $750 per month.

Nowadays, titles recommended in the Frequently Bought Together section are a product of the Amazon algorithm. However, when the "BXGY" option was available to everyone *and* if somebody specifically paid a "BXGY advertising fee" for the space, Amazon would "pair" the purchaser's book with a related (and presumably higher-ranked) book in this space. Amazon would also support the co-op effort by offering a discount if both books (yours and the other book) were purchased at the same time. The discount would come out of Amazon's margin.

Amazon *does* offer the BXGY opportunity to authors who are listing their books via the Amazon Advantage program. If you fall into

Amazon does offer the BXGY opportunity to authors who are listing their books via the Amazon Advantage program.

that category, you can place a nomination for a pairing by logging into your Advantage portal, clicking on "Customer Service," followed by "Select Issue-Coop and Paid Placements," followed by "Select Sub Issue."

Amazon requires full payment for the pairing before the beginning of the month in which the online pairing occurs. BXGY promotions last for one month. Amazon also requires that the requests for pairings be made between one and three months in advance. Acceptance is subject to availability since titles cannot share BXGY months with multiple titles.

SELECTING AN X-TITLE WITH BXGY

It would not make sense to associate yourself with a book that has a sales rank of 2,000 if your book has a sales rank of 700. But if your book has a sales rank of 100,000 and you locate a book in your competitive network that has a sales rank of ten, well, there is a perfect match.

The book with a sales rank of ten is getting a lot of exposure and selling a lot of copies. A lot of people are seeing that book's Detail Page, and a lot of people are buying that book. A certain percentage of them would take advantage of a discount if they were offered one. Enter Amazon and the BXGY promotion. When your book is featured next to that book, consumers can buy both books for a small discount. A moment ago, these shoppers had never heard of your book; but now, thanks to the BXGY program, you are leveraging the value of the popular book to close the sale.

Even if shoppers do not take advantage of the discount, they may click on your cover to learn more about your book. It may stick in their minds and they may come back later to purchase it at a different time.

When you select the book to pair yours with, make sure it appeals to the same audience. It will not do any good to associate yourself with a book that has no appeal to your readers. The success or failure of your BXGY campaign hinges upon making a successful pairing. Amazon makes no guarantees that your sales will increase, and they will take your BXGY fee regardless of whether you sell a lot of books or none at all.

The wisest move, therefore, is to analyze how much you make from each book you sell on Amazon. Once you know that number, ask yourself how many books you must sell to make up the initial investment. If you feel confident that you will sell the required number of copies, the BXGY promotion is a good one, provided you are a member of the Advantage program. It's probably not worth becoming an Advantage member solely for this opportunity, based upon the details outlined in Chapter One and Chapter Seven.

CHAPTER 7
PRICING CONSIDERATIONS

Ultimately, the success you have selling your book on Amazon comes down to time and money—how much time you invest compared to how much money you make. At first, the time investment may far exceed the monetary return as you complete the tactics outlined in this book. Then, as your exposure on Amazon grows, the financial gain may follow suit.

The degree of financial gain is what separates a moderate success from a rousing success. As they say, the devil is in the details. Let us consider two hypothetical books that sell 25,000 copies apiece on

Amazon. One book nets its author $1 per copy while the other book nets its author $2 per copy. What seems like an insignificant difference up close ($1) becomes substantial when multiplied by the total number of book sales.

PRICING & PROFITABILITY

I realize that being an author is mostly a creative endeavor. When subjects such as mathematics, accountability, profitability, and ROI arise, writers have a tendency to tune out. Math is a subject most authors dislike, but it is important to understand basic accounting concepts if you plan on publishing a book profitably.

Of course, analyzing cost assumes you have business interests in mind. If your book is just a hobby, you might not necessarily expect to recoup your investment. After all, hobbies cost money; they don't make money. But the minute your publication becomes a business, or if you hope for it to become a business in the future, then you need to focus on profitability.

Your retail price plays a key role in how many books you are going to sell and how much money you are going to make.

But price analysis is not limited to the retail price. Just as important is the trade discount you set for your book. Different sales channels have different requirements for discounting. You want to set the lowest trade discount possible for the greatest available gain, and that depends upon where you realistically anticipate selling the most books.

Realistically *anticipating* something is different from *hoping* for something. The compromise of those two concepts is what separates a profitable author from an unprofitable one.

Your sales channels, therefore, have the greatest impact on your book's profitability. Various sales channels offer various pricing opportunities. It is best to pick a pricing model that offers the greatest degree of profitability for your book, even if the concept might conflict with your predetermined notions of what book publishing is all about.

The most basic analysis is one involving cost versus profit. How much is it going to cost you to publish your book versus how many books must you sell in order to recoup that investment and start earning a profit?

Similar to the manner in which we started this book, allow me to introduce two different Amazon scenarios: a 55% (standard trade

> It is best to pick a pricing model that offers the greatest degree of profitability for your book, even if the concept might conflict with your predetermined notions of what book publishing is all about.

discount) margin and a 20% (short discount) margin. Let's examine the mathematics involved in selling your book on Amazon via both methods.

★★★   ## THE 55% MARGIN

The Amazon Advantage program introduces a mathematical hurdle immediately—its 55% margin (and the 60% margin for EDC distribution through CreateSpace is even worse). If your book has a retail price of $10.00, Amazon Advantage pays you a wholesale price of $4.50 for a copy of your book. If you deal with Amazon directly, as most Advantage authors do, that $4.50 represents your total gross profit from Amazon.

Out of that $4.50, you have to pay for printing, shipping, and overhead. Printing costs vary considerably depending on how or where you printed your book, but for the sake of this example, we will say you printed 2,500 copies in advance at a cost of $1 each.

Offset printers typically charge a 5%–10% overage fee since the actual print run might be closer to 2,700. You have to pay for those extra copies, too. Once the books are printed, they are typically shipped to your location at your cost.

Yes, if you are an independent self-publisher using Amazon Advantage, you pay for shipping twice—once to ship books from the printer to your location and then again from your location to Amazon. Some printers may offer to ship directly to Amazon for you; if so, determine what their inventory and service fees are. They may be worth their weight in gold.

Depending upon your sales history, Advantage book orders range in quantity from two books at a time to a case, or maybe more. It all depends upon how many books you are selling. Amazon strives to have about three weeks of inventory on hand.

Of course, the costs that are easiest to forget are general and administrative costs. G&A costs include your time, your physical location, the packing and shipping materials, etc. When you receive an order from Amazon via email, you must pack the books along with the packing slip, print a mailing label, calculate the shipping cost, and put the books into the mail. It is neither efficient nor systemized, because it lacks automation. It is too easy to forget about these intangible costs (and most authors do), but they add up quickly.

To disregard your general and administrative costs is to fool yourself into believing your book is more profitable than it actually

General and administrative costs include your time, your location, and shipping materials. Shipping books yourself is rarely cost-effective because it lacks automation.

To disgregard G&A costs is to fool yourself into believing your book is more profitable than it actually is.

is. Remember, the devil is in the details. Let us assume you make $25 an hour and it takes you fifteen minutes to complete an Amazon order. The hourly wage and time expenditure may be higher or lower in your case, but it serves the purpose of providing an example.

Let's say that you mail an average of five books to Amazon every time they request an order. Fifteen minutes at $25/hour is $6.25. If you mail five books at a time, that adds a cost of $1.25 to each book.

Now let us average the overage cost, additional overhead costs, and shipping costs (both to your location and back to Amazon) at $0.75 per book. Add it all up and your total cost for each book is $3.00, including the $1.00 printing cost you began with.

Amazon pays you $4.50 for each book. Your cost for each book is $3.00. Therefore your net profit (before taxes) for each Amazon sale is $1.50. If you earn $25/hour, you must sell 16 books per hour to make up for the amount of time you are spending to sell your book.

To complicate matters further, let's now analyze your book's profitability. Your initial cost of $2,700 for printing 2,700 books requires that you sell 1,800 books to break even if you earn $1.50 each. Once you have sold 1,800 books, you will have 900 books left in your initial print run. At $1.50 for each book, you will make $1,350 profit, assuming all 2,700 books sell.

THE 20% MARGIN

Now let us examine another way of selling a book on Amazon, and that is by *short discounting* through EDI. As you may recall from earlier chapters, EDI stands for Electronic Data Interchange and is available through various book wholesalers, including Ingram. Ingram is the largest book wholesaler in the United States and has direct relationships with Amazon, Barnes & Noble, and countless other book retailers.

In reality, the only way to take advantage of an EDI program through Ingram is to partner with a POD printer or publisher, since Ingram rarely works with independent authors who have published fewer than seven books. On the other hand, many on-demand companies have EDI relationships with Ingram, which results in automatic listings on Amazon, Barnes & Noble, and other popular book retail websites.

The main advantage of EDI distribution is that it is possible to list your book on Amazon for less than a 55% margin. If your larg-

Remember the quote from Dan Poynter: "Bookstores are a lousy place to sell books." Why offer 55% when you can offer as little as 20%?

est sales channel will be online (and for 90% of us, that is the reality), why offer 55% when you can offer as little as 20%? Fifty-five percent margins are for traditional bookstores, not online retailers where computers do the majority of the work. Remember the famous quote from Dan Poynter, author of *The Self-Publishing Manual*: "Bookstores are a lousy place to sell books." Amen.

Let's see how a 20% margin through on-demand and EDI compares with the 55% scenario above. The same $10.00 retail price has a discounted profit of $8.00 per book rather than $4.50.

Of course, the on-demand edition of your book costs more than $1.00 each. It is probably closer to $6.00 each. The good news is, you do not have to pay twice for shipping or any of the general administrative costs, since the on-demand publisher handles fulfillment details for you. Instead you can take the entire difference between $8.00 and $6.00, provided you select the right publisher.

In other words, for every $10.00 book that you sell on Amazon, you net $2.00. No shipping, overhead, or overage fees. In fact, no fulfillment headaches at all. Let's say your upfront cost for the on-demand publishing service is $1,000. Now you have to sell 500 books to break even (rather than 1,800). If you sell an additional 900 books (to remain identical to the first scenario), you clear $1,800 in profit (rather than $1,350).

Higher profits for less work? Authors of the new millennium are discovering what brick and mortar bookstores want to keep a secret: that more profit in less time is a good deal for you and a bad deal for their business model.

Another advantage of publishing on-demand is that your books are listed with both Amazon and Barnes & Noble, whereas if you apply for the Amazon Advantage program, you will not receive a listing on the Barnes & Noble website without expending a duplicate amount of effort. Doing two tasks to accomplish one single goal (online distribution worldwide) is the opposite of digital leverage. In other words, you are working twice as hard with Amazon Advantage for half the online availability.

It is important to find an on-demand publisher that lets you set your own trade discount if you just want to focus on online sales. You also must keep 100% of the difference between the production cost of the book and the amount they receive for selling your book through wholesale. Some publishers pay you a royalty of 10%–20% of the net profit they receive, which means you would be earn-

It is important to find an on-demand publisher that lets you set your own trade discount if you just want to focus on online sales.

Avoid semantics by determining what your profit will be in dollars and cents, not royalty percentages.

ing 10%–20% of $2. Other publishers promote 100% royalties and in most cases, they mean 100% of the profit of the book. Percentages are fuzzy; dollars and cents are not. To avoid semantics altogether, determine what your profit will be in dollars and cents for every book sold on Amazon.

How does EDI make this possible? Electronic Data Interchange is the transfer of data between different companies using computer networks and the Internet. As more and more companies get connected to the Internet, EDI is becoming increasingly important as an efficient mechanism for companies to buy, sell, and trade information. Once the system is set up, computers do the majority of the work. Computers perform tasks with more efficiency than human beings, which enables a much lower margin to be profitable. A lower margin on increased volume is profitability via economy of scale.

Selling a book through EDI results in automatic distribution and listings with all participating retailers simultaneously, including Barnes & Noble, Powell's, Books-A-Million, and countless other online stores.

Unless your book is already distributed through Ingram, you can take advantage of this new book pricing model by publishing an on-demand edition of your book with a POD publisher. The resources at the end of this book may help you.

When it comes to increasing your profitability online, POD is the best-kept secret in publishing, because what is the point of improving Amazon sales if Amazon makes all the money?

Your big opportunity may be right
where you are now.

- Napoleon Hill

CONCLUSION

As Dan Poynter said in the foreword, Amazon is changing everything, even the very conventions that used to be considered unconditional, like deep discounts and returns. By breathing new life into old business models, on-demand publishing companies with EDI distribution tactics are leveling the playing field.

Self-publishing authors and independent presses that embrace its advantages and understand its limitations, successfully use POD to increase author profits. That is what new technology is all about—increasing efficiencies to increase revenues.

If you choose to say good-bye to preconceived notions about standard book industry conventions, you increase the chances of improving your profits when your book sales climb on Amazon.

This book offers many different techniques geared toward increasing your book sales and I guarantee if you do *all* of them as I have described, your sales *will* increase on Amazon. The degree of that increase depends upon your diligence.

The latest rules have yet to be written, although one rule seems set: the old rules no longer apply. That is good news for most of us, because the old rules prevented us from even participating. Now every writer can play the game. May the most knowledgeable authors win.

RESOURCES

I can suggest other resources you may find helpful, depending upon your goals. Throughout this book I referred to one of my other books, *Self-Publishing Simplified*. This is the publishing guide for our company, Outskirts Press. By offering high-quality writing services, publishing packages, and marketing solutions, Outskirts Press has become one of the fastest-growing full-service publishing and marketing author-support companies in the United States. Outskirts Press authors keep all their rights, set their own retail price and discount, and can take full advantage of worldwide online distribution through EDI.

The paperback edition of *Self-Publishing Simplified* is available on Amazon with a suggested retail price of $5.95.

The Kindle edition is available for $0.99.

The e-book edition is free from our website at **outskirtspress.com/selfpublishing.html**

A children's book about how to publish a children's book, *Adventures in Publishing* is intended for authors interested in self-publising a full-color book with full-color illustrations. It is available from Amazon for $9.95.

The e-book edition is free from our website at **outskirtspress.com/selfpublishing.html**

Publishing Gems: Insider Information for the Self-Publishing Writer offers a potpourri of writing, publishing, and promotion advice in convenient list form.

The paperback is available on Amazon for $9.99 and the Kindle edition is $5.00.

For articles and personal comments relating to writing, self-publishing, speaking, marketing, and entrepreneurship, visit my blog at **www.brentsampson.com.**

If you found this book valuable, please let me know by posting a positive review for it on Amazon.com. Don't forget to mention your book in your Personal Headline. Let the promotion begin!

INDEX

LaVergne, TN USA
18 November 2010
205461LV00001B/36/P